GREAT EXPECTATIONS

Charles Dickens

This edition published by Spark Publishing

Spark Publishing
A Division of SparkNotes LLC
120 Fifth Avenue, 8th Floor
New York, NY 10011

Please submit all comments and questions or report errors to www.sparknotes.com/errors

Printed and bound in the United States

ISBN 1-58663-356-2

INTRODUCTION: STOPPING TO BUY SPARKNOTES ON A SNOWY EVENING

Whose words these are you *think* you know.
Your paper's due tomorrow, though;
We're glad to see you stopping here
To get some help before you go.

Lost your course? You'll find it here.
Face tests and essays without fear.
Between the words, good grades at stake:
Get great results throughout the year.

Once school bells caused your heart to quake
As teachers circled each mistake.
Use SparkNotes and no longer weep,
Ace every single test you take.

Yes, books are lovely, dark, and deep,
But only what you grasp you keep,
With hours to go before you sleep,
With hours to go before you sleep.

Contents

CONTEXT

CHARLES DICKENS was born on February 7, 1812, and spent the first nine years of his life living in the coastal regions of Kent, a county in southeast England. Dickens's father, John, was a kind and likable man, but he was incompetent with money and piled up tremendous debts throughout his life. When Dickens was nine, his family moved to London. When he was twelve, his father was arrested and taken to debtors' prison. Dickens's mother moved his seven brothers and sisters into prison with their father, but she arranged for the young Charles to live alone outside the prison and work with other children pasting labels on bottles in a blacking warehouse (blacking was a type of manufactured soot used to make a black pigment for products such as matches or fertilizer). Dickens found the three months he spent apart from his family highly traumatic. Not only was the job itself miserable, but he considered himself too good for it, earning the contempt of the other children. After his father was released from prison, Dickens returned to school. He eventually became a law clerk, then a court reporter, and finally a novelist. His first novel, *The Pickwick Papers,* became a huge popular success when Dickens was only twenty-five. He published extensively and was considered a literary celebrity until his death in 1870.

Many of the events from Dickens's early life are mirrored in *Great Expectations,* which, apart from *David Copperfield,* is his most autobiographical novel. Pip, the novel's protagonist, lives in the marsh country, works at a job he hates, considers himself too good for his surroundings, and experiences material success in London at a very early age, exactly as Dickens himself did. In addition, one of the novel's most appealing characters, Wemmick, is a law clerk, and the law, justice, and the courts are all important components of the story.

Great Expectations is set in early Victorian England, a time when great social changes were sweeping the nation. The Industrial Revolution of the late eighteenth and early nineteenth centuries had transformed the social landscape, enabling capitalists and manufacturers to amass huge fortunes. Although social class was no longer entirely dependent on the circumstances of one's birth, the divisions between rich and poor remained nearly as wide as ever. London, a teeming mass of humanity, lit by gas lamps at night and darkened by black clouds from smokestacks during the day, formed a sharp contrast with the nation's sparsely populated rural areas. More and more people moved from the country to the city in search of greater economic opportunity. Throughout England, the manners of the upper class were very strict and conservative: gentlemen and ladies were expected to have thorough classical educations and to behave appropriately in innumerable social situations.

These conditions defined Dickens's time, and they make themselves felt in almost every facet of *Great Expectations*. Pip's sudden rise from country laborer to city gentleman forces him to move from one social extreme to another while dealing with the strict rules and expectations that governed Victorian England. Ironically, this novel about the desire for wealth and social advancement was written partially out of economic necessity. Dickens's magazine, *All the Year Round*, had become extremely popular based on the success of works it had published in serial, such as his own *A Tale of Two Cities* and Wilkie Collins's *The Woman in White*. But it had experienced a decline in popularity after publishing a dull serial by Charles Lever called *A Day's Ride*. Dickens conceived of *Great Expectations* as a means of restoring his publication's fortunes. The book is still immensely popular a century and a half later.

In form, *Great Expectations* fits a pattern popular in nineteenth-century European fiction: the bildungsroman, or novel depicting growth and personal development, generally a transition from boyhood to manhood such as that experienced by Pip. The genre was popularized by Goethe with his book *Wilhelm Meister* (1794-1796) and became prevalent in England with such books as Daniel Defoe's *Robinson Crusoe*, Charlotte Brontë's *Jane Eyre*, and Dickens's own *David Copperfield*. Each of these works, like *Great Expectations*, depicts a process of maturation and self-discovery through experience as a protagonist moves from childhood to adulthood.

PLOT OVERVIEW

PIP, A YOUNG ORPHAN living with his sister and her husband in the marshes of Kent, sits in a cemetery one evening looking at his parents' tombstones. Suddenly, an escaped convict springs up from behind a tombstone, grabs Pip, and orders him to bring him food and a file for his leg irons. Pip obeys, but the fearsome convict is soon captured anyway. The convict protects Pip by claiming to have stolen the items himself.

One day Pip is taken by his Uncle Pumblechook to play at Satis House, the home of the wealthy dowager Miss Havisham, who is extremely eccentric: she wears an old wedding dress everywhere she goes and keeps all the clocks in her house stopped at the same time. During his visit, he meets a beautiful young girl named Estella, who treats him coldly and contemptuously. Nevertheless, he falls in love with her and dreams of becoming a wealthy gentleman so that he might be worthy of her. He even hopes that Miss Havisham intends to make him a gentleman and marry him to Estella, but his hopes are dashed when, after months of regular visits to Satis House, Miss Havisham tells him that she will help him fill out the papers necessary for him to become a common laborer in his family's business.

With Miss Havisham's guidance, Pip is apprenticed to his brother-in-law, Joe, who is the village blacksmith. Pip works in the forge unhappily, struggling to better his education with the help of the plain, kind Biddy and encountering Joe's malicious day laborer, Orlick. One night, after an altercation with Orlick, Pip's sister, known as Mrs. Joe, is viciously attacked and becomes a mute invalid. From her signals, Pip suspects that Orlick was responsible for the attack.

One day a lawyer named Jaggers appears with strange news: a secret benefactor has given Pip a large fortune, and Pip must come to London immediately to begin his education as a gentleman. Pip happily assumes that his previous hopes have come true—that Miss Havisham is his secret benefactor and that the old woman intends for him to marry Estella.

In London, Pip befriends a young gentleman named Herbert Pocket and Jaggers's law clerk, Wemmick. He expresses disdain for his former friends and loved ones, especially Joe, but he continues to pine after Estella. He furthers his education by studying with the tutor Matthew Pocket, Herbert's father. Herbert himself helps Pip learn how to act like a gentleman. When Pip turns twenty-one and begins to receive an income from his fortune, he will secretly help Herbert buy his way into the business he has chosen for himself. But for now, Herbert and Pip lead a fairly undisciplined life in London, enjoying themselves and running up debts. Orlick reappears in Pip's life, employed as Miss Havisham's porter, but is promptly fired by Jaggers after Pip reveals Orlick's unsavory past. Mrs. Joe dies, and Pip goes home for the funeral, feeling tremendous grief and remorse. Several years go by, until one night a familiar figure barges into Pip's room—the convict, Magwitch, who stuns Pip by announcing that he, not Miss Havisham, is the source of Pip's fortune. He tells Pip that he was so moved by Pip's boyhood kindness that he dedicated his life to making Pip a gentleman, and he made a fortune in Australia for that very purpose.

Pip is appalled, but he feels morally bound to help Magwitch escape London, as the convict is pursued both by the police and by Compeyson, his former partner in crime. A complicated mystery begins to fall into place when Pip discovers that Compeyson was the man who abandoned Miss Havisham at the altar and that Estella is Magwitch's daughter. Miss Havisham has raised her to break men's hearts, as revenge for the pain her own broken heart caused her. Pip was merely a boy for the young Estella to practice on; Miss Havisham delighted in Estella's ability to toy with his affections.

As the weeks pass, Pip sees the good in Magwitch and begins to care for him deeply. Before Magwitch's escape attempt, Estella marries an upper-class lout named Bentley Drummle. Pip makes a visit to Satis House, where Miss Havisham begs his forgiveness for the way she has treated him in the past, and he forgives her. Later that day, when she bends over the fireplace, her clothing catches fire and she goes up in flames. She survives but becomes an invalid. In her final days, she will continue to repent for her misdeeds and to plead for Pip's forgiveness.

The time comes for Pip and his friends to spirit Magwitch away from London. Just before the escape attempt, Pip is called to a shadowy meeting in the marshes, where he encounters the vengeful, evil Orlick. Orlick is on the verge of killing Pip when Herbert arrives with a group of friends and saves Pip's life. Pip and Herbert hurry back to effect Magwitch's escape. They try to sneak Magwitch down the river on a rowboat, but they are discovered by the police, who Compeyson tipped off. Magwitch and Compeyson fight in the river, and Compeyson is drowned. Magwitch is sentenced to death, and Pip loses his fortune. Magwitch feels that his sentence is God's forgiveness and dies at peace. Pip falls ill; Joe comes to London to care for him, and they are reconciled. Joe gives him the news from home: Orlick, after robbing Pumblechook, is now in jail; Miss Havisham has died and left most of her fortune to the Pockets; Biddy has taught Joe how to read and write. After Joe leaves, Pip decides to rush home after him and marry Biddy, but when he arrives there he discovers that she and Joe have already married.

Pip decides to go abroad with Herbert to work in the mercantile trade. Returning many years later, he encounters Estella in the ruined garden at Satis House. Drummle, her husband, treated her badly, but he is now dead. Pip finds that Estella's coldness and cruelty have been replaced by a sad kindness, and the two leave the garden hand in hand, Pip believing that they will never part again. (NOTE: Dickens's original ending to *Great Expectations* differed from the one described in this summary. The final Summary and Analysis section of this SparkNote provides a description of the first ending and explains why Dickens rewrote it.)

CHARACTER LIST

Pip The protagonist and narrator of Great Expectations, Pip begins the story as a young orphan boy being raised by his sister and brother-in-law in the marsh country of Kent, in the southeast of England. Pip is passionate, romantic, and somewhat unrealistic at heart, and he tends to expect more for himself than is reasonable. Pip also has a powerful conscience, and he deeply wants to improve himself, both morally and socially.

Estella Miss Havisham's beautiful young ward, Estella is Pip's unattainable dream throughout the novel. He loves her passionately, but, though she sometimes seems to consider him a friend, she is usually cold, cruel, and uninterested in him. As they grow up together, she repeatedly warns him that she has no heart.

Miss Havisham Miss Havisham is the wealthy, eccentric old woman who lives in a manor called Satis House near Pip's village. She is manic and often seems insane, flitting around her house in a faded wedding dress, keeping a decaying feast on her table, and surrounding herself with clocks stopped at twenty minutes to nine. As a young woman, Miss Havisham was jilted by her fiancé minutes before her wedding, and now she has a vendetta against all men. She deliberately raises Estella to be the tool of her revenge, training her beautiful ward to break men's hearts.

Abel Magwitch ("The Convict") A fearsome criminal, Magwitch escapes from prison at the beginning of Great Expectations and terrorizes Pip in the cemetery. Pip's kindness, however, makes a deep impression on him, and he subsequently devotes himself to making a fortune and using it to elevate Pip into a higher social class. Behind the scenes, he becomes Pip's secret benefactor, funding Pip's education and opulent lifestyle in London through the lawyer Jaggers.

CHARACTER LIST

Joe Gargery Pip's brother-in-law, the village blacksmith, Joe stays with his overbearing, abusive wife—known as Mrs. Joe—solely out of love for Pip. Joe's quiet goodness makes him one of the few completely sympathetic characters in Great Expectations. Although he is uneducated and unrefined, he consistently acts for the benefit of those he loves and suffers in silence when Pip treats him coldly.

Jaggers The powerful, foreboding lawyer hired by Magwitch to supervise Pip's elevation to the upper class. As one of the most important criminal lawyers in London, Jaggers is privy to some dirty business; he consorts with vicious criminals, and even they are terrified of him. But there is more to Jaggers than his impenetrable exterior. He often seems to care for Pip, and before the novel begins he helps Miss Havisham to adopt the orphaned Estella. Jaggers smells strongly of soap: he washes his hands obsessively as a psychological mechanism to keep the criminal taint from corrupting him.

Herbert Pocket Pip first meets Herbert Pocket in the garden of Satis House, when, as a pale young gentleman, Herbert challenges him to a fight. Years later, they meet again in London, and Herbert becomes Pip's best friend and key companion after Pip's elevation to the status of gentleman. Herbert nicknames Pip "Handel." He is the son of Matthew Pocket, Miss Havisham's cousin, and hopes to become a merchant so that he can afford to marry Clara Barley.

Wemmick Jaggers's clerk and Pip's friend, Wemmick is one of the strangest characters in Great Expectations. At work, he is hard, cynical, sarcastic, and obsessed with "portable property"; at home in Walworth, he is jovial, wry, and a tender caretaker of his "Aged Parent."

Biddy A simple, kindhearted country girl, Biddy first befriends Pip when they attend school together. After Mrs. Joe is attacked and becomes an invalid, Biddy moves into Pip's home to care for her. Throughout most of the novel, Biddy represents the opposite of Estella; she is plain, kind, moral, and of Pip's own social class.

Dolge Orlick The day laborer in Joe's forge, Orlick is a slouching, oafish embodiment of evil. He is malicious and shrewd, hurting people simply because he enjoys it. He is responsible for the attack on Mrs. Joe, and he later almost succeeds in his attempt to murder Pip.

Mrs. Joe Pip's sister and Joe's wife, known only as "Mrs. Joe" throughout the novel. Mrs. Joe is a stern and overbearing figure to both Pip and Joe. She keeps a spotless household and frequently menaces her husband and her brother with her cane, which she calls "Tickler." She also forces them to drink a foul-tasting concoction called tar-water. Mrs. Joe is petty and ambitious; her fondest wish is to be something more than what she is, the wife of the village blacksmith.

Uncle Pumblechook Pip's pompous, arrogant uncle. (He is actually Joe's uncle and, therefore, Pip's "uncle-in-law," but Pip and his sister both call him "Uncle Pumblechook.") A merchant obsessed with money, Pumblechook is responsible for arranging Pip's first meeting with Miss Havisham. Throughout the rest of the novel, he will shamelessly take credit for Pip's rise in social status, even though he has nothing to do with it, since Magwitch, not Miss Havisham, is Pip's secret benefactor.

Compeyson A criminal and the former partner of Magwitch, Compeyson is an educated, gentlemanly outlaw who contrasts sharply with the coarse and uneducated Magwitch. Compeyson is responsible for Magwitch's capture at the end of the novel. He is also the man who jilted Miss Havisham on her wedding day.

Bentley Drummle An oafish, unpleasant young man who attends tutoring sessions with Pip at the Pockets' house, Drummle is a minor member of the nobility, and the sense of superiority this gives him makes him feel justified in acting cruelly and harshly toward everyone around him. Drummle eventually marries Estella, to Pip's chagrin; she is miserable in their marriage and reunites with Pip after Drummle dies some eleven years later.

Molly Jaggers's housekeeper. In Chapter 48, Pip realizes that she is Estella's mother.

Mr. Wopsle The church clerk in Pip's country town; Mr. Wopsle's aunt is the local schoolteacher. Sometime after Pip becomes a gentleman, Mr. Wopsle moves to London and becomes an actor.

Startop A friend of Pip's and Herbert's. Startop is a delicate young man who, with Pip and Drummle, takes tutelage with Matthew Pocket. Later, Startop helps Pip and Herbert with Magwitch's escape.

Miss Skiffins Wemmick's beloved, and eventual wife.

ANALYSIS OF MAJOR CHARACTERS

PIP

As a bildungsroman, *Great Expectations* presents the growth and development of a single character, Philip Pirrip, better known to himself and to the world as Pip. As the focus of the bildungsroman, Pip is by far the most important character in *Great Expectations*: he is both the protagonist, whose actions make up the main plot of the novel, and the narrator, whose thoughts and attitudes shape the reader's perception of the story. As a result, developing an understanding of Pip's character is perhaps the most important step in understanding *Great Expectations*.

Because Pip is narrating his story many years after the events of the novel take place, there are really two Pips in *Great Expectations*: Pip the narrator and Pip the character—the voice telling the story and the person acting it out. Dickens takes great care to distinguish the two Pips, imbuing the voice of Pip the narrator with perspective and maturity while also imparting how Pip the character feels about what is happening to him as it actually happens. This skillfully executed distinction is perhaps best observed early in the book, when Pip the character is a child; here, Pip the narrator gently pokes fun at his younger self, but also enables us to see and feel the story through his eyes.

As a character, Pip's two most important traits are his immature, romantic idealism and his innately good conscience. On the one hand, Pip has a deep desire to improve himself and attain any possible advancement, whether educational, moral, or social. His longing to marry Estella and join the upper classes stems from the same idealistic desire as his longing to learn to read and his fear of being punished for bad behavior: once he understands ideas like poverty, ignorance, and immorality, Pip does not want to be poor, ignorant, or immoral. Pip the narrator judges his own past actions extremely harshly, rarely giving himself credit for good deeds but angrily castigating himself for bad ones. As a character, however, Pip's idealism often leads him to perceive the world rather narrowly, and his tendency to oversimplify situations based on superficial values leads him to behave badly toward the people who care about him. When Pip becomes a gentleman, for example, he immediately begins to act as he thinks a gentleman is supposed to act, which leads him to treat Joe and Biddy snobbishly and coldly.

On the other hand, Pip is at heart a very generous and sympathetic young man, a fact that can be witnessed in his numerous acts of kindness throughout the book (helping Magwitch, secretly buying Herbert's way into business, etc.) and his essential love for all those who love him. Pip's main line of development in the novel may be seen as the process of learning to place his innate sense of kindness and conscience above his immature idealism.

Not long after meeting Miss Havisham and Estella, Pip's desire for advancement largely overshadows his basic goodness. After receiving his mysterious fortune, his idealistic wishes seem to have been justified, and he gives himself over to a gentlemanly life of idleness. But the discovery that the wretched Magwitch, not the wealthy Miss Havisham, is his secret benefactor shatters Pip's oversimplified sense of his world's hierarchy. The fact that he comes to admire Magwitch while losing Estella to the brutish nobleman Drummle ultimately forces him to realize that one's social position is not the most important quality one possesses, and that his behavior as a gentleman has caused him to hurt the people who care about him most. Once he has learned these lessons, Pip matures into the man who narrates the novel, completing the bildungsroman.

ESTELLA

Often cited as Dickens's first convincing female character, Estella is a supremely ironic creation, one who darkly undermines the notion of romantic love and serves as a bitter criticism against the class system in which she is mired. Raised from the age of three by Miss Havisham to torment men and "break their hearts," Estella wins Pip's deepest love by practicing deliberate cruelty. Unlike the warm, winsome, kind heroine of a traditional love story, Estella is cold, cynical, and manipulative. Though she represents Pip's first longed-for ideal of life among the upper classes, Estella is actually even lower-born than Pip; as Pip learns near the end of the novel, she is the daughter of Magwitch, the coarse convict, and thus springs from the very lowest level of society.

Ironically, life among the upper classes does not represent salvation for Estella. Instead, she is victimized twice by her adopted class. Rather than being raised by Magwitch, a man of great inner nobility, she is raised by Miss Havisham, who destroys her ability to express emotion and interact normally with the world. And rather than marrying the kindhearted commoner Pip, Estella marries the cruel nobleman Drummle, who treats her harshly and makes her life miserable for many years. In this way, Dickens uses Estella's life to reinforce the idea that one's happiness and well-being are not deeply connected to one's social position: had Estella been poor, she might have been substantially better off.

Despite her cold behavior and the damaging influences in her life, Dickens nevertheless ensures that Estella is still a sympathetic character. By giving the reader a sense of her inner struggle to discover and act on her own feelings rather than on the imposed motives of her upbringing, Dickens gives the reader a glimpse of Estella's inner life, which helps to explain what Pip might love about her. Estella does not seem able to stop herself from hurting Pip, but she also seems not to want to hurt him; she repeatedly warns him that she has "no heart" and seems to urge him as strongly as she can to find happiness by leaving her behind. Finally, Estella's long, painful marriage to Drummle causes her to develop along the same lines as Pip—that is, she learns, through experience, to rely on and trust her inner feelings. In the final scene of the novel, she has become her own woman for the first time in the book. As she says to Pip, "Suffering has been stronger than all other teaching. . . . I have been bent and broken, but—I hope—into a better shape."

MISS HAVISHAM

The mad, vengeful Miss Havisham, a wealthy dowager who lives in a rotting mansion and wears an old wedding dress every day of her life, is not exactly a believable character, but she is certainly one of the most memorable creations in the book. Miss Havisham's life is defined by a single tragic event: her jilting by Compeyson on what was to have been their wedding day. From that moment forth, Miss Havisham is determined never to move beyond her heartbreak. She stops all the clocks in Satis House at twenty minutes to nine, the moment when she first learned that Compeyson was gone, and she wears only one shoe, because when she learned of his betrayal, she had not yet put on the other shoe. With a kind of manic, obsessive cruelty, Miss Havisham adopts Estella and raises her as a weapon to achieve her own revenge on men. Miss Havisham is an example of single-minded vengeance pursued destructively: both Miss Havisham and the people in her life suffer greatly because of her quest for revenge. Miss Havisham is completely unable to see that her actions are hurtful to Pip and Estella. She is redeemed at the end of the novel when she realizes that she has caused Pip's heart to be broken in the same manner as her own; rather than achieving any kind of personal revenge, she has only caused more pain. Miss Havisham immediately begs Pip for forgiveness, reinforcing the novel's theme that bad behavior can be redeemed by contrition and sympathy.

THEMES, MOTIFS & SYMBOLS

THEMES

Themes are the fundamental and often universal ideas explored in a literary work.

AMBITION AND SELF-IMPROVEMENT

The moral theme of *Great Expectations* is quite simple: affection, loyalty, and conscience are more important than social advancement, wealth, and class. Dickens establishes the theme and shows Pip learning this lesson, largely by exploring ideas of ambition and self-improvement—ideas that quickly become both the thematic center of the novel and the psychological mechanism that encourages much of Pip's development. At heart, Pip is an idealist; whenever he can conceive of something that is better than what he already has, he immediately desires to obtain the improvement. When he sees Satis House, he longs to be a wealthy gentleman; when he thinks of his moral shortcomings, he longs to be good; when he realizes that he cannot read, he longs to learn how. Pip's desire for self-improvement is the main source of the novel's title: because he believes in the possibility of advancement in life, he has "great expectations" about his future.

Ambition and self-improvement take three forms in *Great Expectations*—moral, social, and educational; these motivate Pip's best and his worst behavior throughout the novel. First, Pip desires moral self-improvement. He is extremely hard on himself when he acts immorally and feels powerful guilt that spurs him to act better in the future. When he leaves for London, for instance, he torments himself about having behaved so wretchedly toward Joe and Biddy. Second, Pip desires social self-improvement. In love with Estella, he longs to become a member of her social class, and, encouraged by Mrs. Joe and Pumblechook, he entertains fantasies of becoming a gentleman. The working out of this fantasy forms the basic plot of the novel; it provides Dickens the opportunity to gently satirize the class system of his era and to make a point about its capricious nature. Significantly, Pip's life as a gentleman is no more satisfying—and certainly no more moral—than his previous life as a blacksmith's apprentice. Third, Pip desires educational improvement. This desire is deeply connected to his social ambition and longing to marry Estella: a full education is a requirement of being a gentleman. As long as he is an ignorant country boy, he has no hope of social advancement. Pip understands this fact as a child, when he learns to read at Mr. Wopsle's aunt's school, and as a young man, when he takes lessons from Matthew Pocket. Ultimately, through the examples of Joe, Biddy, and Magwitch, Pip learns that social and educational improvement are irrelevant to one's real worth and that conscience and affection are to be valued above erudition and social standing.

SOCIAL CLASS

Throughout *Great Expectations,* Dickens explores the class system of Victorian England, ranging from the most wretched criminals (Magwitch) to the poor peasants of the marsh country (Joe and Biddy) to the middle class (Pumblechook) to the very rich (Miss Havisham). The theme of social class is central to the novel's plot and to the ultimate moral theme of the book—Pip's realization that wealth and class are less important than affection, loyalty, and inner worth. Pip achieves this realization when he is finally able to understand that, despite the esteem in which he holds Estella, one's social status is in no way connected to one's real character. Drummle, for instance, is an upper-class lout, while Magwitch, a persecuted convict, has a deep inner worth.

Perhaps the most important thing to remember about the novel's treatment of social class is that the class system it portrays is based on the post-Industrial Revolution model of Victorian England. Dickens generally ignores the nobility and the hereditary aristocracy in favor of characters whose fortunes have been earned through commerce. Even Miss Havisham's family fortune was made through the brewery that is still connected to her manor. In this way, by connecting the theme of social class to the idea of work and self-advancement, Dickens subtly reinforces the novel's overarching theme of ambition and self-improvement.

CRIME, GUILT, AND INNOCENCE

The theme of crime, guilt, and innocence is explored throughout the novel largely through the characters of the convicts and the criminal lawyer Jaggers. From the handcuffs Joe mends at the smithy to the gallows at the prison in London, the imagery of crime and criminal justice pervades the book, becoming an important symbol of Pip's inner struggle to reconcile his own inner moral conscience with the institutional justice system. In general, just as social class becomes a superficial standard of value that Pip must learn to look beyond in finding a better way to live his life, the external trappings of the criminal justice system (police, courts, jails, etc.) become a superficial standard of morality that Pip must learn to look beyond to trust his inner conscience. Magwitch, for instance, frightens Pip at first simply because he is a convict, and Pip feels guilty for helping him because he is afraid of the police. By the end of the book, however, Pip has discovered Magwitch's inner nobility, and is able to disregard his external status as a criminal. Prompted by his conscience, he helps Magwitch to evade the law and the police. As Pip has learned to trust his conscience and to value Magwitch's inner character, he has replaced an external standard of value with an internal one.

MOTIFS

Motifs are recurring structures, contrasts, or literary devices that can help to develop and inform the text's major themes.

DOUBLES

One of the most remarkable aspects of Dickens's work is its structural intricacy and remarkable balance. Dickens's plots involve complicated coincidences, extraordinarily tangled webs of human relationships, and highly dramatic developments in which setting, atmosphere, event, and character are all seamlessly fused.

In *Great Expectations,* perhaps the most visible sign of Dickens's commitment to intricate dramatic symmetry—apart from the knot of character relationships, of course—is the fascinating motif of doubles that runs throughout the book. From the earliest scenes of the novel to the last, nearly every element of *Great Expectations* is mirrored or doubled at some other point in the book. There are two convicts on the marsh (Magwitch and Compeyson), two invalids (Mrs. Joe and Miss Havisham), two young women who interest Pip (Biddy and Estella), and so on. There are two secret benefactors: Magwitch, who gives Pip his fortune, and Pip, who mirrors Magwitch's action by secretly buying Herbert's way into the mercantile business. Finally, there are two adults who seek to mold children after their own purposes: Magwitch, who wishes to "own" a gentleman and decides to make Pip one, and Miss Havisham, who raises Estella to break men's hearts in revenge for her own broken heart. Interestingly, both of these actions are motivated by Compeyson: Magwitch resents but is nonetheless covetous of Compeyson's social status and education, which motivates his desire to make Pip a gentleman, and Miss Havisham's heart was broken when Compeyson left her at the altar, which motivates her desire to achieve revenge through Estella. The relationship between Miss Havisham and Compeyson—a well-born woman and a common man—further mirrors the relationship between Estella and Pip.

This doubling of elements has no real bearing on the novel's main themes, but, like the connection of weather and action, it adds to the sense that everything in Pip's world is connected. Throughout Dickens's works, this kind of dramatic symmetry is simply part of the fabric of his novelistic universe.

COMPARISON OF CHARACTERS TO INANIMATE OBJECTS

Throughout *Great Expectations*, the narrator uses images of inanimate objects to describe the physical appearance of characters—particularly minor characters, or characters with whom the narrator is not intimate. For example, Mrs. Joe looks as if she scrubs her face with a nutmeg grater, while the inscrutable features of Mr. Wemmick are repeatedly compared to a letter-box. This motif, which Dickens uses throughout his novels, may suggest a failure of empathy on the narrator's part, or it may suggest that the character's position in life is pressuring them to resemble a thing more than a human being. The latter interpretation would mean that the motif in general is part of a social critique, in that it implies that an institution such as the class system or the criminal justice system dehumanizes certain people.

SYMBOLS

Symbols are objects, characters, figures, or colors used to represent abstract ideas or concepts.

SATIS HOUSE

In Satis House, Dickens creates a magnificent Gothic setting whose various elements symbolize Pip's romantic perception of the upper class and many other themes of the book. On her decaying body,

Miss Havisham's wedding dress becomes an ironic symbol of death and degeneration. The wedding dress and the wedding feast symbolize Miss Havisham's past, and the stopped clocks throughout the house symbolize her determined attempt to freeze time by refusing to change anything from the way it was when she was jilted on her wedding day. The brewery next to the house symbolizes the connection between commerce and wealth: Miss Havisham's fortune is not the product of an aristocratic birth but of a recent success in industrial capitalism. Finally, the crumbling, dilapidated stones of the house, as well as the darkness and dust that pervade it, symbolize the general decadence of the lives of its inhabitants and of the upper class as a whole.

THE MISTS ON THE MARSHES
The setting almost always symbolizes a theme in *Great Expectations* and always sets a tone that is perfectly matched to the novel's dramatic action. The misty marshes near Pip's childhood home in Kent, one of the most evocative of the book's settings, are used several times to symbolize danger and uncertainty. As a child, Pip brings Magwitch a file and food in these mists; later, he is kidnapped by Orlick and nearly murdered in them. Whenever Pip goes into the mists, something dangerous is likely to happen. Significantly, Pip must go through the mists when he travels to London shortly after receiving his fortune, alerting the reader that this apparently positive development in his life may have dangerous consequences.

BENTLEY DRUMMLE
Although he is a minor character in the novel, Bentley Drummle provides an important contrast with Pip and represents the arbitrary nature of class distinctions. In his mind, Pip has connected the ideas of moral, social, and educational advancement so that each depends on the others. The coarse and cruel Drummle, a member of the upper class, provides Pip with proof that social advancement has no inherent connection to intelligence or moral worth. Drummle is a lout who has inherited immense wealth, while Pip's friend and brother-in-law Joe is a good man who works hard for the little he earns. Drummle's negative example helps Pip to see the inner worth of characters such as Magwitch and Joe, and eventually to discard his immature fantasies about wealth and class in favor of a new understanding that is both more compassionate and more realistic.

SYMBOLS

Summary & Analysis

Chapters 1–3

Summary: Chapter 1

As an infant, Philip Pirrip was unable to pronounce either his first name or his last; doing his best, he called himself "Pip," and the name stuck. Now Pip, a young boy, is an orphan living in his sister's house in the marsh country in southeast England.

One evening, Pip sits in the isolated village churchyard, staring at his parents' tombstones. Suddenly, a horrific man, growling, dressed in rags, and with his leg in chains, springs out from behind the gravestones and seizes Pip. This escaped convict questions Pip harshly and demands that Pip bring him food and a file with which he can saw away his leg irons.

Summary: Chapter 2

Frightened into obedience, Pip runs to the house he shares with his overbearing sister and her kindly husband, the blacksmith Joe Gargery. The boy stashes some bread and butter in one leg of his pants, but he is unable to get away quickly. It is Christmas Eve, and Pip is forced to stir the holiday pudding all evening. His sister, whom Pip calls Mrs. Joe, thunders about. She threatens Pip and Joe with her cane, which she has named Tickler, and with a foul-tasting concoction called tar-water. Very early the next morning, Pip sneaks down to the pantry, where he steals some brandy (mistakenly refilling the bottle with tar-water, though we do not learn this until Chapter 4) and a pork pie for the convict. He then sneaks to Joe's smithy, where he steals a file. Stealthily, he heads back into the marshes to meet the convict.

Summary: Chapter 3

Unfortunately, the first man he finds hiding in the marshes is actually a second, different convict, who tries to strike Pip and then flees. When Pip finally comes upon his original tormentor, he finds him suffering, cold, wet, and hungry. Pip is kind to the man, but the convict becomes violent again when Pip mentions the other escapee he encountered in the marsh, as though the news troubles him greatly.

As the convict scrapes at his leg irons with the file, Pip slips away through the mists and returns home.

_____

ANALYSIS: CHAPTERS 1–3

The first chapters of *Great Expectations* set the plot in motion while introducing Pip and his world. As both narrator and protagonist, Pip is naturally the most important character in *Great Expectations*: the novel is his story, told in his words, and his perceptions utterly define the events and characters of the book. As a result, Dickens's most important task as a writer in *Great Expectations* is the creation of Pip's character. Because Pip's is the voice with which he tells his story, Dickens must make his voice believably human while also ensuring that it conveys all the information necessary to the plot. In this first section, Pip is a young child, and Dickens masterfully uses Pip's narration to evoke the feelings and problems of childhood. At the beginning of the novel, for instance, Pip is looking at his parents' gravestones, a solemn scene which Dickens renders comical by having Pip ponder the exact inscriptions on the tombstones. When the convict questions him about his parents' names, Pip recites them exactly as they appear on the tombstones, indicating his youthful innocence while simultaneously allowing Dickens to lessen the dramatic tension of the novel's opening.

As befits a well-meaning child whose moral reasoning is unsophisticated, Pip is horrified by the convict. But despite his horror, he treats him with compassion and kindness. It would have been easy for Pip to run to Joe or to the police for help rather than stealing the food and the file, but Pip honors his promise to the suffering man— and when he learns that the police are searching for him, he even worries for his safety. Still, throughout this section, Pip's self-commentary mostly emphasizes his negative qualities: his dishonesty and his guilt. This is characteristic of Pip as a narrator throughout *Great Expectations*. Despite his many admirable qualities—the strongest of which are compassion, loyalty, and conscience—Pip constantly focuses on his failures and shortcomings. To understand him as a character, it is necessary to look beyond his self-descriptions and consider his actions. In fact, it may be his powerful sense of his own moral shortcomings that motivates Pip to act so morally. As the novel progresses, the theme of self-improvement, particularly economic and social self-improvement, will become central to the story. In that sense, Pip's deep-seated sense of moral obligation, which is first exhibited in this section, works as a kind of psychological counterpart to the novel's theme of social advancement.

Pip's surroundings—in this section, the "shrouded" marshes of Kent and the oppressive bustle of Mrs. Joe's house—are also important to the novel. Throughout *Great Expectations*, Dickens uses setting to create dramatic atmosphere: the setting of the book always sets the tone for the action and reinforces Pip's perception of his situation. When the weather is dark and stormy, trouble is usually brewing, and when Pip goes alone into the mist-shrouded marsh, danger and ambiguity usually await. In this section, Pip's story shifts rapidly between dramatic scenes with the convict on the marshes and comical scenes under Mrs. Joe's thumb at home. Despite Mrs. Joe's rough treatment of Pip, which she calls bringing him up "by hand," the comedy that pervades her household in Chapter 2 shows that it is a safe haven for Pip, steeped in Joe's quiet goodness despite Mrs. Joe's bombast. When Pip ventures out alone onto the marshes, he leaves the sanctuary of home for vague, murky churchyards and the danger of a different world. This sense of embarking alone into the unknown will become a recurrent motif throughout the novel, as Pip grows up and leaves his childhood home behind.

In terms of narrative, the introduction of the convict is the most important occurrence in the plot of the first section. Though Pip believes that the convict's appearance in his life is an isolated incident, he will feel this character's influence in many ways throughout the novel. The convict will later reappear as the grim Magwitch, Pip's secret benefactor and the chief architect of his "great expectations." Though Dickens gives us no indication of the man's future in Pip's life, he does create the sense that the convict will return, largely by building a sense of mystery around the man's situation and around his relationship to the second convict Pip encounters in the marsh.

CHAPTERS 4–7

SUMMARY: CHAPTER 4

As he returns home, Pip is overwhelmed by a sense of guilt for having helped the convict. He even expects to find a policeman waiting for him at Joe's house. When Pip slips into the house, he finds no policemen, only Mrs. Joe busy in the kitchen cooking Christmas dinner. Pip eats breakfast alone with Joe. The two go to church; Mrs. Joe, despite her moralizing habits, stays behind.

Christmas dinner is an agonizing affair for Pip, who is crowded into a corner of the table by his well-to-do Uncle Pumblechook and the church clerk, Mr. Wopsle. Terrified that his sneaking out of the house to help the convict will be discovered, Pip nearly panics when Pumblechook asks for the brandy and finds the bottle filled with tar-water. His panic increases when, suddenly, several police officers burst into the house with a pair of handcuffs.

SUMMARY: CHAPTER 5

> *My convict looked round him for the first time, and saw me. . . .*
>
> (See QUOTATIONS, p. 57)

Pip is sure that the policemen have come to arrest him, but all they want is for Joe to fix their handcuffs. The bumbling policemen tell Pip and Joe that they are searching for a pair of escaped convicts, and the two agree to participate in the manhunt. Seeing the policemen, Pip feels a strange surge of worry for "his" convict.

After a long hunt, the two convicts are discovered together, fighting furiously with one another in the marsh. Cornered and captured, Pip's convict protects Pip by claiming to have stolen the food and file himself. The convict is taken away to a prison ship and out of Pip's life—so Pip believes—forever.

SUMMARY: CHAPTER 6

Joe carries Pip home, and they finish their Christmas dinner; Pip sleepily heads to bed while Joe narrates the scene of the capture to Mrs. Joe and the guests. Pip continues to feel powerfully guilty about the incident—not on his sister's account, but because he has not told the whole truth to Joe.

SUMMARY: CHAPTER 7

After the incident, some time passes. Pip lives with his guilty secret and struggles to learn reading and writing at Mrs. Wopsle's school. At school, Pip befriends Biddy, the granddaughter of the teacher. One day, Joe and Pip sit talking; the illiterate Joe admires a piece of writing Pip has just done. Suddenly, Mrs. Joe bursts in with Pumblechook. Highly self-satisfied, they reveal that Pumblechook has arranged for Pip to go play at the house of Miss Havisham, a rich spinster who lives nearby. Mrs. Joe and Pumblechook hope she will make Pip's fortune, and they plan to send him home with Pumblechook before he goes to Miss Havisham's the next day. The boy is given a rough bath, dressed in his suit, and taken away by Pumblechook.

ANALYSIS: CHAPTERS 4–7

In addition to the introduction of the convict, the other important plot development in the early chapters of *Great Expectations* occurs at the very end of Chapter 7, when Pip learns he is to be taken to Miss Havisham's to play. His introduction to Miss Havisham and her world will determine a great part of his story and will change him forever. Though Pip has no sense of the importance of the event, Dickens conveys its importance to the reader through Mrs. Joe and Pumblechook, who are obviously ecstatic at the idea of Pip befriending the wealthy old woman. This is the first hint in the novel of the theme of social class and social improvement, which will quickly become the dominant idea.

Because he spends the first several chapters of the book exclusively among those of his own social station, the theme of social class is not particularly important in this section. But Pip's low social standing makes itself felt in subtle ways—in the colloquial dialect spoken by Joe and his sister, the mean ambition of Mrs. Joe and Pumblechook, and the ineffective rigor of his country school (where he is taught by Mr. Wopsle's great aunt), for example. By describing Pip's early education, Dickens continues to emphasize the idea of self-improvement. Just as Pip's behavior indicates a desire for moral improvement and Mrs. Joe's ambition indicates a desire for social improvement, Pip's struggle to learn to read indicates a desire for intellectual and educational improvement. To emphasize this point, Dickens contrasts Pip's meager knowledge with the ignorance of Joe, who admires Pip's poor writing because he is unable to read or write himself.

Dickens also uses this scene to develop Pip's special relationship with Joe. Although Joe is not Pip's father or even his brother, he is the most caring person in his life—a simple, honest man. Dickens contrasts Joe's earnest good nature with the grasping ambition and self-satisfaction of Pumblechook and Mrs. Joe, implying even at this early stage of the novel that real self-improvement (the kind that leads to goodness) is not connected to social advancement or even education, but rather stems from honesty, empathy, and kindness. Pip will spend fifty chapters learning this lesson himself, and will then be struck by the fact that, in the figure of Joe, the best example had been in front of him all along.

As he did in the first three chapters, throughout this section Dickens demonstrates a masterful ability to tell his story effectively without ever losing the perspective of childhood. Though the novel itself is narrated by the adult Pip remembering his life, Pip the character is still a little boy in these chapters, and the narrator comically and sympathetically conveys his immature impressions. At the Christmas dinner in Chapter 4, for instance, Pip is terrified that his secret will be found out, but he balances his fear with a deep desire to tweak Mr. Wopsle's large nose—to "pull it until he howled." His sense of guilt for sneaking behind his guardians' backs is so great that he believes the whole world is busy trying to discover his secret, and he fully expects to "find a constable in the kitchen, waiting to take me up."

CHAPTERS 8–10

SUMMARY: CHAPTER 8

Over breakfast the next morning, Pumblechook sternly grills Pip on multiplication problems. At ten, he is taken to Miss Havisham's manor, Satis House. The gate is locked, and a small, very beautiful girl comes to open it. She is rude to Pumblechook and sends him away when she takes Pip inside. She leads him through the ornate, dark mansion to Miss Havisham's candlelit room, where the skeletal old woman waits by her mirror, wearing a faded wedding dress, surrounded by clocks stopped at twenty minutes to nine.

The girl leaves, and Miss Havisham orders Pip to play. He tells her earnestly that he is too affected by the newness and grandeur of the house to play. Miss Havisham forces him to call for the girl, whose name is Estella. Estella returns, and Miss Havisham orders her to play cards with Pip. Estella is cold and insulting, criticizing Pip's low social class and his unrefined manners. Miss Havisham is morbidly delighted to see that Pip is nonetheless taken with the girl. Pip cries when he leaves Satis House.

SUMMARY: CHAPTER 9

When Pip returns home, he lies to Joe, Mrs. Joe, and Pumblechook about his experience at Satis House, inventing a wild story in which Estella feeds him cake and four immense dogs fight over veal cutlet from a silver basket. He feels guilty for lying to Joe and tells him the truth in the smithy later that day. Joe, who is astonished to find out that Pip has lied, advises Pip to keep company with his own class for the present and tells him that he can succeed someday only if he takes an honest path. Pip resolves to remember Joe's words, but that night, as he lies in bed, he can't help but imagine how "common" Estella would find Joe, and he falls into a reverie about the grandeur of his hours at Satis House.

SUMMARY: CHAPTER 10

Pip continues to suffer through his schooling, but a new desire for education and social standing makes him agree to take extra lessons from his sensible friend Biddy. Later the same day, when Pip goes to the pub to bring Joe home, he sees a mysterious stranger stirring his drink with the same file Pip stole for the convict. The stranger gives Pip two pounds, which Pip later gives to Mrs. Joe. He continues to worry that his aid to the convict will be discovered.

ANALYSIS: CHAPTERS 8–10

With the introduction of Miss Havisham and Estella, the themes of social class, ambition, and advancement move to the forefront of the novel. Pip's hopes (encouraged by Mrs. Joe's and Pumblechook's suggestive comments) that Miss Havisham intends to raise him into wealth and high social class are given special urgency by the passionate attraction he feels for Estella. His feelings for the "very pretty and very proud" young lady, combined with the deep impression made on him by Satis House, with its ornate grandeur, haunted atmosphere, and tragic sense of mystery, raise in Pip a new consciousness of his own low birth and common bearing. When he returns from Satis House in Chapter 9, he even lies about his experience there, unwilling to sully his thoughts of it with the contrasting plainness of his everyday world: Estella and Miss Havisham must remain "far above the level of such common doings."

Pip's romantic sensibility, first visible in his tendency to linger around his parents' gravestones, is powerfully attracted to the enigmatic world of Satis House. His desire for self-improvement compels him to idealize Estella. Her condescension and spite match Pip's feelings about himself in the world of Satis House. He accepts her cruelty—"Why, he is a common labouring-boy!"—without defending himself because he sorrowfully believes her to be right. In fact, he only cries when he is forced to leave her. The differences between their social classes manifest themselves even in small things; while playing cards in Chapter 8, Estella remarks disdainfully, "He calls the knaves, jacks, this boy!"

Though the introduction of Satis House and Miss Havisham seem to have little to do with the early plotline of the convict and the marshes, Dickens keeps the earlier story in the reader's mind with the appearance of the mysterious figure in Chapter 10, who stirs his drink with the file Pip gave to the convict and gives Pip a small sum of money. This foreshadows not only the eventual return of the convict, but also the major plot twist of the novel, when Pip discovers that the source of his mysterious fortune (which he has not yet received in this section) is not Miss Havisham, as he thought, but the convict Magwitch.

Like the earlier chapters, this section abounds in mystery and foreshadowing, particularly relating to Miss Havisham's character: what is the reason behind her bizarre appearance, her behavior, and her home decor, with its stopped clocks and crumbling relics of an earlier time? At this stage of the novel, Dickens does not answer questions, only raises them. The reader's natural curiosity will help propel the book forward.

CHAPTERS 11–13

SUMMARY: CHAPTER 11
Not long after his encounter with the mysterious man in the pub, Pip is taken back to Miss Havisham's, where he is paraded in front of a group of fawning, insincere relatives visiting the dowager on her birthday. He encounters a large, dark man on the stairs, who criticizes him. He again plays cards with Estella, then goes to the garden, where he is asked to fight by a pale young gentleman. Pip knocks the young gentleman down, and Estella allows him to give her a kiss on the cheek. He returns home, ashamed that Estella looks down on him.

SUMMARY: CHAPTER 12
Pip worries that he will be punished for fighting, but the incident goes unmentioned during his next visit to Miss Havisham's. He continues to visit regularly for the next several months, pushing Miss Havisham around in her wheelchair, relishing his time with Estella, and becoming increasingly hopeful that Miss Havisham means to raise him from his low social standing and give him a gentleman's fortune. Because he is preoccupied with his hopes, he fails to notice

that Miss Havisham encourages Estella to torment him, whispering "Break their hearts!" in her ear. Partially because of his elevated hopes for his own social standing, Pip begins to grow apart from his family, confiding in Biddy instead of Joe and often feeling ashamed that Joe is "common." One day at Satis House, Miss Havisham offers to help with the papers that would officially make Pip Joe's apprentice, and Pip is devastated to realize that she never meant to make him a gentleman.

SUMMARY: CHAPTER 13

Joe visits Satis House to complete Pip's apprenticeship papers; with his rough speech and crude appearance, he seems horribly out of place in the Gothic mansion. Estella laughs at him and at Pip. Miss Havisham gives Pip a gift of twenty-five pounds, and Pip and Joe go to Town Hall to confirm the apprenticeship. Joe and Mrs. Joe take Pip out to celebrate with Pumblechook and Mr. Wopsle, but Pip is surly and angry, keenly disappointed by this turn in his life.

ANALYSIS: CHAPTERS 11–13

Where the earlier sections of the novel focused very closely on short spans of time, this section covers several months and is mostly concerned with Pip's general development from an innocent boy to an ambitious young man. The themes of ambition and social advancement are central to this development, as Pip increasingly uses his ambiguous relationship with Miss Havisham as a pretext for believing that the old woman intends him to marry Estella. The consequence of Pip's intensifying social ambition is that he loses some of his innocence and becomes detached from his natural, sympathetic kindness. In the early chapters of the novel, Pip sympathized with the convict, despite the threat the man posed to his safety. Now, Pip is unable to sympathize even with Joe, the most caring figure in his life. Because he loves Estella, Pip has come to value what Estella seems to value, and when Joe visits Satis House in Chapter 13, Pip is mortified by his rough manners and poor clothes. They now seem out of place even to Pip, a measure of the extent to which he has adapted to life at Miss Havisham's house during his months of regular visits.

Miss Havisham herself, with her maniacal energy and her inscrutable motives, is a frightening creature to Pip. Despite her wedding dress (an outfit that symbolizes hope, regeneration, and renewal), he constantly thinks of her as a symbol of death, describing her as a "skeleton" and picturing her hanging from a gallows. Her insane behavior—traipsing around her house in a wedding dress, with a wedding feast on her table and all the clocks stopped—will soon be explained, but for now it simply adds to her mysterious and powerful dramatic presence. Surely a woman this eccentric wouldn't be above transforming an orphan boy into a gentleman, he thinks. With this line of thinking, the first of Pip's "great expectations" creeps into his life.

The title of the novel, of course, refers to Pip's hopes for social advancement and romantic success with Estella. The sight of something finer than what he himself has makes him intensely desire it, and he fiercely clings to his hopes of being elevated and married to Estella. He even ignores more realistic hopes, using his relationship with Biddy only to improve his education and his chances with Estella. He has little reaction to realistic dangers, as we saw earlier, when he was nonplussed by his encounter with the mysterious stranger in Chapter 10. His thoughts are for Estella alone.

Athough Pip increasingly believes that Miss Havisham intends to make him a gentleman (at least until his disappointment in Chapter 13), Dickens creates dramatic irony by giving the reader a sense that the old woman has no such intention in mind. Rather, Dickens indicates that Miss Havisham is not really interested in Pip at all but only in somehow using Estella as a weapon against men. As the novel progresses, the source of her strange hostility will become clear, but in this section of the novel the reader is already able to make a fairly good guess: jilted on her wedding day (hence the dress and the feast), the old woman has raised Estella as a tool of revenge on men, training her to break men's hearts as her own heart was broken years ago. Throughout this section, unbeknownst to him, Pip is her test case, an experiment to measure the young girl's prowess at winning the love of men. Toward this purpose, Miss Havisham is delighted by the speed with which Pip falls in love with Estella.

Pip's realization that the extent of Miss Havisham's assistance will be her help on his apprenticeship papers—that he will be bound to Joe's forge and to his social class after all—is devastating to him; it is the first of a series of disappointments that seem to be the inevitable result of Pip's great expectations.

Chapters 14–16

Summary: Chapter 14

Time passes as Pip begins working in Joe's forge; the boy slowly becomes an adolescent. He hates working as Joe's apprentice, but out of consideration for Joe's goodness, he keeps his feelings to himself. As he works, he thinks he sees Estella's face mocking him in the forge, and he longs for Satis House.

Summary: Chapter 15

Pip still tries hard to read and expand his knowledge, and on Sundays, he also tries to teach Joe to read. One Sunday, Pip tries to persuade Joe that he needs to visit Miss Havisham, but Joe again advises him to stay away. However, his advice sounds confused, and Pip resolves to do as he pleases.

Joe's forge worker, Dolge Orlick, makes Pip's life even less pleasant. Orlick is vicious, oafish, and hateful, and he treats Pip cruelly. When Pip was still a young child, Orlick frightened him by convincing him that the devil lived in a corner of the forge. One day, Mrs. Joe complains about Orlick taking a holiday, and she and Orlick launch into a shouting match. Mrs. Joe gleefully calls on Joe to defend her honor, and Joe quickly defeats Orlick in the fight. Mrs. Joe faints from excitement.

Pip visits Miss Havisham and learns that Estella has been sent abroad. Dejected, he allows Wopsle to take him to Pumblechook's for the evening, where they pass the time reading from a play. On the way home, Pip sees Orlick in the shadows and hears guns fire from the prison ships. When he arrives home, he learns that Mrs. Joe has been attacked and is now a brain-damaged invalid.

Summary: Chapter 16

Pip's old guilt resurfaces when he learns that convicts—more specifically, convicts with leg irons that have been filed through—are suspected of the attack on his sister. The detectives who come from London to solve the crime are bumblers, and the identity of the attacker remains undiscovered. Mrs. Joe, who is now unable to talk, begins to draw the letter "T" on her slate over and over, which Pip guesses represents a hammer. From this, Biddy deduces that she is referring to Orlick. Orlick is called in to see Mrs. Joe, and Pip expects her to denounce him as her attacker. Instead, she seems eager to please Orlick and often calls for him in subsequent days by drawing a "T" on her slate.

ANALYSIS: CHAPTERS 14–16

In Chapter 10, Pip received an unwelcome reminder of the convict when the stranger in the pub appeared with the stolen file. In this section, he receives an even more unpleasant reminder when an escaped convict from the prison ships—possibly the stranger from the pub—is blamed for the attack on Mrs. Joe. Because of Pip's powerful moral sense, he is racked with guilt over the incident. As he says in Chapter 16, "It was horrible to think that I had provided the instrument, however undesignedly." Of course, Mrs. Joe's strange interest in Orlick in the next chapters marks him as the true attacker, and Pip guesses this truth almost immediately. Even though Pip is in no way at fault in the incident, his conscience still troubles him.

Themes of guilt and innocence run powerfully through this section, as Pip's adolescent mind wavers between right and wrong, between his desire to be good and his stark sense of evil. The play he reads at Pumblechook's house tells the story of a man whose lover convinces him to kill his uncle for money. Pip will soon abandon Joe for money and the promise of Estella. Like the apparition of the convict and the figures of the police, the fight between Joe and Orlick emphasizes this theme of starkly divided good and evil: Orlick's slouching, lumbering badness is a powerful contrast to Joe's quiet inner goodness, and their fight gives a physical presence to Pip's internal struggle.

CHAPTERS 17–19

SUMMARY: CHAPTER 17

Biddy moves in to help nurse Mrs. Joe. Pip visits Satis House again and notices how bleak it is without Estella. He walks with Biddy on Sunday and confides to her his dissatisfaction with his place in life. Although he seems to be attracted to Biddy, he tells her the secret of his love for Estella. When Biddy advises him to stay away from Estella, Pip is angry with her, but he still becomes very jealous when Orlick begins trying to flirt with her.

SUMMARY: CHAPTER 18

At the pub one evening, Pip sits in a crowd listening to Wopsle read the story of a murder trial from a newspaper. A stranger begins questioning Wopsle about the legal details of the case. Pip recognizes him as the large, dark man he met on the stairs at Miss Havisham's (in Chapter 11). The stranger introduces himself as the lawyer Jaggers, and he goes home with Pip and Joe. Here, he explains that Pip will soon inherit a large fortune. His education as a gentleman will begin immediately. Pip will move to London and become a gentleman, he says, but the person who is giving him the fortune wishes to remain secret: Pip can never know the name of his benefactor.

Pip's fondest wish has been realized, and he assumes that his benefactor must be Miss Havisham—after all, he first met Jaggers at her house, and his tutor will be Matthew Pocket, her cousin. Joe seems deflated and sad to be losing Pip, and he refuses Jaggers's condescending offer of money. Biddy is also sad, but Pip adopts a snobbish attitude and thinks himself too good for his surroundings. Still, when Pip sees Joe and Biddy quietly talking together that night, he feels sorry to be leaving them.

SUMMARY: CHAPTER 19

Pip's snobbery is back in the morning, however, as he allows the tailor to grovel over him when he goes in for a new suit of clothes. Pip even allows Pumblechook to take him out to dinner and ingratiate himself. He tries to comfort Joe, but his attempt is obviously forced, and Biddy criticizes him for it. Preparing to leave for London, he visits Miss Havisham one last time; based on her excitement and knowledge of the details of his situation, Pip feels even more certain that she is his anonymous benefactor. After a final night at Joe's house, Pip leaves for London in the morning, suddenly full of regret for having behaved so snobbishly toward the people who love him most.

ANALYSIS: CHAPTERS 17–19

As Pip enters adolescence, Dickens gradually changes the presentation of his thoughts and perceptions. When Pip was a young child, his descriptions emphasized his smallness and confusion; beginning around Chapter 14, they begin to emphasize his moral and emotional turmoil. Pip becomes more aware of the qualities and characteristics of the people around him. He refrains from complaining about life in the forge out of respect for Joe's role in his childhood: "Home was never a pleasant place for me, because of my sister's temper. But Joe had sanctified it." Though the respect he pays Joe is clearly admirable, Pip the narrator passes to Joe all the credit for his behavior. He says in Chapter 14, "It was not because I was faithful, but because Joe was faithful."

Just as Orlick is an immediate contrast to Joe, Biddy emerges in this section as a contrasting figure to Estella. Her plainness, frankness, and kindness are diametrically opposed to Estella's cold beauty, dishonesty, and cruelty. Pip seems to feel a natural attraction to Biddy, but his overpowering passion for Estella makes him use Biddy only as a means to an end, as a confidante and a teacher.

Pip's desire to elevate his social standing never leaves him; he even seeks to better his surroundings by trying to teach Joe to read. When the ominous figure of the lawyer Jaggers appears with the message of Pip's sudden fortune, the young man's deepest wish comes true. But the exultant Pip is not content simply to enjoy his good fortune; rather, he reads more into it than he should, deciding that "Miss Havisham intended me for Estella" and that she must be his benefactor. His adolescent self-importance causes him to put on airs and act snobbishly toward Joe and Biddy, a character flaw that Pip will demonstrate throughout *Great Expectations*. In his career as a gentleman, he will cover up moments of uncertainty and fear by acting, as he says in Chapter 19, "virtuous and superior."

In part, this poor behavior is caused by the same character trait that causes Pip to covet self-advancement. Pip has a deep-seated strain of romantic idealism, and as soon as he can imagine something better than his current condition (whether material, emotional, or moral), he immediately desires that improvement: when he sees Satis House, he longs for wealth; when he meets Estella, he longs for love and beauty; and when he acts poorly, he feels a powerful guilt that amounts to a longing to have acted more morally. This is the psychological center of the novel's theme of self-improvement. But Pip's romantic idealism is inherently unrealistic. Whatever he might wish, it is impossible to become a gentleman overnight and never again be a common boy, to immediately forget one's old friends, family, and surroundings, and to abruptly change one's inner self.

When Pip suddenly receives his fortune, he experiences a moment in which his romantic ideal seems to have come true. But the impediments remain, and Pip is forced to contend with the entanglements of his affection for his family and his home. Feeling his emotions clash, Pip is unsure how to behave, so he gives in fully to his romantic side and tries to act like a wealthy aristocrat—a person, he imagines, who would be snobbish to Joe and Biddy. Though he is at heart a very good person, Pip has not yet learned to value human affection and loyalty above his immature vision of how the world ought to be. In this section and throughout the novel, behaving snobbishly is a way for Pip to simplify the complicated emotional situations in which he finds himself as he attempts to impose his immature picture of the world on the real complexities of life.

When Pip moves to London, a new stage in his life begins. As we are told at the end of Chapter 19: "This is the end of the first stage of Pip's expectations."

CHAPTERS 20–26

SUMMARY: CHAPTER 20
Jaggers takes Pip to London, where the country boy is amazed and displeased by the stench and the thronging crowds in such areas as Smithfield. Jaggers seems to be an important and powerful man: hordes of people wait outside his office, muttering his name among themselves. Pip meets Jaggers's cynical, wry clerk, Wemmick.

SUMMARY: CHAPTER 21
Wemmick introduces Pip to Herbert Pocket, the son of Pip's tutor, with whom Pip will spend the night. Herbert and Pip take an immediate liking to one another; Herbert is cheerful and open, and Pip feels that his easy good nature is a contrast to his own awkward diffidence. Whereas Pip's fortune has been made for him, Herbert is an impoverished gentleman who hopes to become a shipping merchant. They realize, surprised, that they have met before: Herbert is the pale young gentleman whom Pip fought in the garden at Satis House.

SUMMARY: CHAPTER 22
Pip asks Herbert to help him learn to be a gentleman, and, after a feast, the two agree to live together. Herbert subtly corrects Pip's poor table manners, gives him the nickname "Handel," and tells him the whole story of Miss Havisham. When she was young, her family fortune was misused by her unruly half brother, and she fell in love with—and agreed to marry—a man from a lower social class than her own. This man convinced her to buy her half brother's share of the family brewery, which he wanted to run, for a huge price. But on their wedding day, the man never appeared, instead sending a note which Miss Havisham received at twenty minutes to nine—the time at which she later stopped all her clocks. It was assumed that Miss Havisham's lover was in league with her half brother and that they split the profits from the brewery sale. At some later point, Miss Havisham adopted Estella, but Herbert does not know when or where.

SUMMARY: CHAPTER 23

The next day, Pip visits the unpleasant commercial world of the Royal Exchange before going to Matthew Pocket's house to be tutored and to have dinner. The Pockets' home is a bustling, chaotic place where the servants run the show. Matthew is absentminded but kind, and his wife is socially ambitious but not well born; the children are being raised by the nurse. Pip's fellow students are a strange pair: Bentley Drummle, a future baronet, is oafish and unpleasant, and a young man named Startop is soft and delicate. At dinner, Pip concentrates on his table manners and observes the peculiarities of the Pockets' social lives.

SUMMARY: CHAPTER 24

Pip returns to Jaggers's office in order to arrange to share rooms with Herbert. There Pip befriends the lively Wemmick, who invites him to dinner. Pip sees Jaggers in the courtroom, where he is a potent and menacing force, frightening even the judge with his thundering speeches.

SUMMARY: CHAPTER 25

Pip continues to get to know his fellow students and the Pockets, attending dinners at both Wemmick's and Jaggers's. Wemmick's house is like something out of a dream, an absurd "castle" in Walworth that he shares with his "Aged Parent." Pip observes that Wemmick seems to have a new personality when he enters his home: while he is cynical and dry at work, at home he seems jovial and merry.

SUMMARY: CHAPTER 26

By contrast, Jaggers's house is oppressive and dark, shared only with a gloomy housekeeper, Molly. Pip's fellow students attend the dinner at Jaggers's with Pip, and Pip and Drummle quarrel over a loan Drummle ungratefully borrowed from Startop. Jaggers warns Pip to stay away from Drummle, though the lawyer claims to like the disagreeable young man himself.

ANALYSIS: CHAPTERS 20–26

Structurally, this series of brief, quick chapters inaugurates the second phase of *Great Expectations*, marked by Pip's receiving his new fortune and his move from Kent to London. Pip's move to London marks a drastic shift of setting for the second main section of *Great Expectations*, away from the desolate marshes of Kent and into the teeming crowds of the city. Dickens, with his consummate knowledge of the London of his era, evokes the city masterfully, describing the stink, the run-down buildings, and the colorful mass of humanity through Pip's stunned perceptions. One of the first things Pip sees after his arrival in London is the terrible gallows of Newgate Prison, which gives Pip "a sickening idea of London." In a novel that places so much emphasis on the relationship between character and setting, it should come as no surprise that Pip encounters objects of punishment and justice everywhere he looks. Beneath his awkward desire to be a gentleman and advance socially, Pip is obsessed with ideas of guilt, innocence, and moral obligation, going all the way back to his first encounter with the convict in the marsh. The gallows evokes not only the memory of the convict, but also the themes of guilt and innocence that preoccupy Pip's young mind.

Pip's new acquaintances are unlike anyone he has ever known before, and they make his transformation into a gentleman an unpredictable one. Jaggers is hard, cold, and powerful, but beneath the surface he seems disgusted by his own work. In Chapter 20, he does not allow his clients to talk to him, and he scrubs his hands ferociously at the end of each workday, symbolically attempting to remove the moral taint of his work. Herbert (the "pale young gentleman" of Chapter 11) makes a natural contrast to the lawyer; he is everything Jaggers is not. Kind, relaxed, and poor, he is the perfect gentleman to educate Pip in the ways of the upper class. Herbert's father, Matthew, is kind as well, but his absentminded carelessness makes him a weak figure even in his own household. Of his students, Drummle is an oaf and Startop is a weakling. Wemmick's split personality—he acts hard and cynical in Jaggers's office but wry and merry at home in Walworth—confuses Pip, but it also emphasizes the inner goodness beneath Wemmick's callous exterior. His insistence on obtaining "portable property" and his good-natured teasing of his "Aged Parent" give him two of his most memorable catchphrases, which he uses throughout the novel.

The story of Miss Havisham mirrors some of the same themes—social class, romantic anguish, and criminality—that run throughout the main story of the book. The story explains the main mystery of Miss Havisham's life, which was implied by her surroundings and her behavior much earlier in the novel. It answers many of Pip's questions about her but raises many more. Who were the criminals who preyed on her, and what became of them? What is Estella's history, and how is she related to Miss Havisham? As the novel progresses, these questions will become extremely important; for now, they are used primarily to continue the sense of mystery that is so important to the forward momentum of Dickens's plot.

CHAPTERS 27–35

SUMMARY: CHAPTER 27

Joe comes to visit Pip in London. Because Pip worries that Joe will disapprove of his opulent lifestyle and that Drummle will look down on him because of Joe, Joe's visit is strained and awkward. He tries to tell Pip the news from home: Wopsle, for instance, has become an actor. But Pip acts annoyed with him until Joe mentions that Estella has returned to Satis House and that she wishes to see Pip. Pip suddenly feels more kindly toward Joe, but the blacksmith leaves before Pip can improve his behavior.

> *"Pip, dear old chap, life is made of ever so many*
> *partings welded together, as I may say, and one man's a*
> *blacksmith, and one's a whitesmith, and one's a*
> *goldsmith, and one's a coppersmith. Divisions among*
> *such must come. . . ."*
>
> *(See* QUOTATIONS, *p. 58)*

SUMMARY: CHAPTER 28

Hoping to see Estella and to apologize to Joe, Pip travels home, forced to share a coach with a pair of convicts, one of whom is the mysterious stranger who gave Pip money in the pub. Though this man does not recognize Pip, Pip overhears him explaining that the convict Pip helped that long-ago night in the marshes had asked him to deliver the money to Pip. Pip is so terrified by his memory of that night that he gets off the coach at its first stop within the town limits. When he arrives at his hotel, he reads a notice in a newspaper, from which he learns that Pumblechook is taking credit for his rise in status.

SUMMARY: CHAPTER 29

When he travels to Satis House the next day, Pip pictures himself as a triumphant knight riding to rescue the Lady Estella from an evil castle. He encounters Orlick, now Miss Havisham's porter, at the gate. When he sees Estella, he is stunned: she has become a ravishing young woman. Despite his newfound fortune, Pip feels horribly inadequate around her, as unworthy and clumsy as ever. Miss Havisham goads him on, snapping at him to continue to love Estella. Pip walks with Estella in the garden, but she treats him with indifference, and he becomes upset. Pip realizes that she reminds him of someone, but he can't place the resemblance. Back inside, he discovers Jaggers there and feels oppressed by the lawyer's heavy presence.

SUMMARY: CHAPTER 30

The next day, Pip tells Jaggers about Orlick's past, and Jaggers fires the man from Miss Havisham's employ. Pip is mocked by the tailor's apprentice as he walks down the street. He returns in low spirits to London, where Herbert tries to cheer him up, though he also tries to convince him that, even if Miss Havisham is his secret benefactor, she does not intend for him to marry Estella. Herbert confesses to Pip that he, too, is in love and, in fact, has a fiancée named Clara, but he is too poor to marry her.

SUMMARY: CHAPTER 31

Pip and Herbert go to the theater, where Wopsle plays a ridiculous Hamlet. Pip takes the hapless actor out to dinner following the play, but his mood remains sour.

SUMMARY: CHAPTER 32

Pip receives a note from Estella, ordering him to meet her at a London train station. He arrives very early and encounters Wemmick, who takes him on a brief tour of the miserable grounds of Newgate Prison. Pip feels uncomfortable in the dismal surroundings, but Wemmick is oddly at home, even introducing Pip to a man who has been sentenced to death by hanging.

SUMMARY: CHAPTER 33

When Pip meets Estella, he is again troubled by her resemblance to someone he can't place. She treats Pip arrogantly, but sends him into ecstatic joy when she refers to their "instructions," which makes him feel as though they are destined to be married. After he escorts her through the gaslit London night to the house at which she is staying, he returns to the Pockets' home.

SUMMARY: CHAPTER 34

Pip feels terribly guilty for his snobbish treatment of Joe and Biddy, and he feels as though his degenerate lifestyle has been a bad influence on Herbert. The two young men catalog their debts, but they are interrupted by a letter carrying the news that Mrs. Joe has died.

SUMMARY: CHAPTER 35

Pip is surprised by the intensity of his sadness about his sister's death. He returns home at once for the funeral. He meets Pumblechook, who continues to fawn over him irritatingly. He tries to mend his relations with Joe and Biddy; Biddy is skeptical of his pledges to visit more often. Pip says goodbye to them the next morning, truly intending to visit more often, and walks away into the mist.

ANALYSIS: CHAPTERS 27–35

These chapters cover a dark and humiliating time for Pip. Ironically, Pip's dizzying rise in social status is accompanied by a sharp decline in his confidence and happiness. He is humiliated in no fewer than four important scenes in this section. First, Joe's visit to London reintroduces the theme of social contrast, showing just how awkward Pip's position between the social classes has become; he worries both that Joe will disapprove of his new life and that the figures in his new life will disapprove of Joe. Second, he is frightened by the convicts in the coach, who remind him of his childhood encounter on the marsh. Third, even his return home is keenly embarrassing, as he learns of Pumblechook's false boast and finds himself mocked by the tailor's apprentice in Chapter 30. And, fourth, most painful of all, what he hopes will be a triumphant return to Satis House as a gentleman is a complete failure: Estella treats him just as cruelly as ever, reminding him coldly that she has "no heart."

Pip's behavior throughout this period is not admirable: he treats Joe with barely disguised hostility during Joe's visit to London, and he behaves haughtily and coldly throughout this section. The difference between Pip the character and Pip the narrator becomes clear here. When he visits Satis House, Pip the character feels irritated and unhappy at the thought of visiting Joe, but Pip the narrator judges himself harshly for having felt that way, writing "God forgive me!" in Chapter 29. As a character, Pip is in the grip of his immediate emotions, but as a narrator, he has the capacity to look at his life from a broader perspective and to judge himself. Dickens uses that contrast well, giving Pip the wisdom of hindsight without sacrificing the immediacy of his story.

Pip's guilt over his behavior toward Joe and Biddy reaches a high point at Mrs. Joe's funeral. He is stunned by the news of his sister's death. More than anyone else except for Joe, Mrs. Joe raised Pip, and her death marks an important point in his maturation toward adulthood and the development of his character. He tries to rectify his behavior toward his lower-class loved ones, but they are skeptical of his promises to improve, and with good reason. Pip really does mean to visit them more, as he promises Biddy in Chapter 35, but when he leaves, he walks into the rising mists, which symbolize ambiguity and confusion throughout *Great Expectations*; even he knows he is unlikely to honor his promise.

Mr. Wopsle's rise as an actor works as a sort of parody of Pip's rise as a gentleman. The country churchman is as ridiculous onstage in Chapter 31 as Pip feels on the street when Trabb, the tailor's boy, mocks him. Another important contrast to Pip in this section is Herbert, whose practical dream of becoming a merchant, earning money, and marrying Clara is virtually the opposite of Pip's fairy-tale rise in status and his irrational belief that Miss Havisham means for him to marry Estella.

CHAPTERS 36–37

SUMMARY: CHAPTER 36
Pip's twenty-first birthday finally arrives, meaning that he is an adult and will begin to receive a regular income from his fortune rather than having to go to Jaggers to access his money. He feels a great sense of excitement, because he hopes that his entrance into adulthood will cause Jaggers to tell him the identity of his mysterious benefactor. Despite Herbert's warning, he feels increasingly certain that it is Miss Havisham and that she means for him to marry Estella. But during their interview, Jaggers is cold and brief; he reveals nothing about the source of Pip's fortune, simply telling him that his income will be five hundred pounds a year and refusing to take responsibility for the outcome. For some reason, the encounter reminds Pip of his meeting with the convict in the graveyard so many years before. Still, Pip invites Jaggers to participate in his birthday dinner, but Jaggers's oppressive presence makes the evening less enjoyable for Pip and Herbert.

SUMMARY: CHAPTER 37
Upon receiving his income, Pip decides to help Herbert by buying Herbert's way into the merchant business. He asks Wemmick for advice. At Jaggers's office (in Chapter 36), Wemmick cynically advises Pip not to help Herbert, but later, at the Castle (where Pip also meets Wemmick's girlfriend, Miss Skiffins), he jovially offers

exactly the opposite advice and agrees to help Pip with the scheme. They find a merchant in need of a young partner, and Pip buys Herbert the partnership. Everything is all arranged anonymously, so that Herbert, like Pip, does not know the identity of his benefactor.

ANALYSIS: CHAPTERS 36–37

Pip's twenty-first birthday marks his official transition to adulthood (Jaggers even begins calling him "Mr. Pip"). Jaggers's refusal to comply with Pip's wishes to know the truth about his benefactor is a bad omen, one borne out in the next section with the arrival of the convict and the downfall of Pip's greatest expectations.

Even though Pip is still self-critical, he has legitimately matured into early adulthood and developed more sympathetic qualities. His decision to use his large income to help Herbert—being "very desirous," as he says, "to serve a friend"—allows him to share his good fortune with a friend in need. Ironically, Pip adopts secrecy even as he is most anxious to know the identity of his own secret benefactor. Of course, he still believes his benefactor to be Miss Havisham, and he even accounts for Jaggers's refusal to talk with the ridiculous deduction that "Miss Havisham had not taken him into her confidence as to her designing me for Estella; that he resented this, and felt a jealousy about it." That Pip imagines the hard, powerful Jaggers feeling jealousy over anything involving Pip illustrates the extent to which Pip must delude himself to believe that Miss Havisham truly intends for him to marry Estella. It is obvious to the reader and to all the other characters in the book that Miss Havisham has no such idea in mind, but Pip remains blinded by love and continues to equate his social advancement with romantic advancement.

This section also continues to develop the character of Wemmick. The bizarre clerk's two distinct sides become even more sharply divided in this section, as office-Wemmick advises Pip not to help Herbert, while Walworth-Wemmick wholeheartedly endorses the plan. Wemmick even acknowledges the split, saying in Chapter 36 that "my Walworth sentiments must be taken at Walworth; none but my official sentiments can be taken at this office." Pip's introduction to Miss Skiffins, Wemmick's girlfriend (and future bride), in Chapter 37 allows Dickens to make an even more sentimental character out of Wemmick, but it also highlights Pip's own romantic troubles. His love for Estella remains desperately impractical, and, as the next section demonstrates, his relationship with her has become humiliating in an entirely new way.

CHAPTERS 38–39

SUMMARY: CHAPTER 38

Pip spends a great deal of time with Estella in the house of her London hostess, Mrs. Brandley. However, he is not treated as a serious suitor. Rather, he is allowed to accompany Estella everywhere she goes, watching her treat her other suitors cruelly but being more or less ignored himself. He cannot understand why Miss Havisham does not announce the details of their engagement, in which he continues to believe. Pip and Estella go to visit the old woman, and Pip observes for the first time a combative relationship between her and Estella: Miss Havisham goads Estella on to break men's hearts, but Estella treats Miss Havisham as coldly as she treats her suitors. Shortly thereafter, Pip learns to his horror that Drummle is courting Estella. He confronts Estella about the news, but she refuses to take his concern seriously, reminding Pip that he is the only suitor she doesn't try to deceive and entrap. But this only makes Pip feel less important to her. That night, the young man imagines his fate as a heavy stone slab hanging over his head, about to fall.

> "I begin to think," said Estella, in a musing way, after another moment of calm wonder, "that I almost understand how this comes about."
>
> *(See* QUOTATIONS, *p. 59)*

SUMMARY: CHAPTER 39

Time passes, and Pip is now twenty-three. One night, during a midnight thunderstorm, he hears heavy footsteps trudging up his stairs. An old sailor enters Pip's apartment, and Pip treats him nervously and haughtily before recognizing him. It is Pip's convict, the same man who terrorized him in the cemetery and on the marsh when he was a little boy. Horrified, Pip learns the truth of his situation: the convict went to Australia, where he worked in sheep ranching and earned a huge fortune. Moved by Pip's kindness to him on the marsh, he arranged to use his wealth to make Pip a gentleman. The convict, not Miss Havisham, is Pip's secret benefactor. Pip is not meant to marry Estella at all.

With a crestfallen heart, Pip hears that the convict is even now on the run from the law, and that if he is caught, he could be put to death. Pip realizes that though the convict's story has plunged him into despair, it is his duty to help his benefactor. He feeds him and gives him Herbert's bed for the night, since Herbert is away. Terrified of his new situation, Pip looks in on the convict, who is sleeping with a pistol on his pillow, and then locks the doors and falls asleep. He awakes at five o'clock in the morning to a dark sky tormented by wind and rain.

ANALYSIS: CHAPTERS 38–39

As we saw in the previous section, Pip has now matured into an adult, marking a new phase in the novel; additionally, the reappearance of the convict and the solution of the mystery of Pip's benefactor mark an important milestone in the book's narrative development. Appropriately, the second important stage of the novel concludes at the end of this section; we are told here, "This is the end of the second stage of Pip's expectations."

Dickens opens this section by illustrating the extent to which Pip must now fool himself to believe that he is still meant to marry Estella. His relationship with Estella has gone from bad to worse: where he was once her innocent playmate, he is now expected to act as her innocuous companion, accompanying her to meet suitor after suitor at innumerable parties, essentially functioning as her chaperone. Dickens contrasts Pip's romantic quandary with the romantic optimism of his friends, who all seem to find romantic happiness. Wemmick has Miss Skiffins and Herbert has Clara; Pip has only the bitter knowledge that the oafish Drummle has begun courting his beloved Estella.

Of course, the most important and most ominous development in these chapters, foreshadowed countless times in the earlier sections of the novel, is the reappearance of the convict, now a rugged old man, and the revelation that he, not Miss Havisham, is Pip's secret benefactor. This revelation deflates Pip's hopes that he is meant for Estella, and it completely collapses the stark social divisions that have defined him in the novel, first as a poor laborer envious of the rich, then as a gentleman embarrassed of his poor relations. Now Pip learns that his wealth and social standing come from the labor of an uneducated prison inmate, turning his social perceptions inside out. The fulfillment of his hope of being raised to a higher social class turns out to be the work of a man from a class even lower than his own. The sense of duty that compels Pip to help the convict is a mark of his inner goodness, just as it was many years ago in the swamp, but he is nevertheless unable to hide his disgust and disappointment.

"Look'ee here, Pip. I'm your second father. You're my son—more to me nor any son. I've put away money, only for you to spend."

(See QUOTATIONS, *p. 61)*

The convict's reference to himself as Pip's "second father" in Chapter 39 allows us to track Pip's development through a succession of father figures. The orphaned Pip identifies most closely with Joe as a father in the first section of the novel, and the blacksmith's soft-spoken good nature most strongly defines his childhood. After the magical appearance of his wealth, adolescent Pip seems to treat Jaggers as a kind of distant father figure, referring to him repeatedly as "my guardian" and allowing him to set the parameters for his life in London. Now a young adult, Pip is confronted with the convict as an unwanted father, a relationship that will develop and deepen in the final section of the novel. With Pip's discovery of his new father figure, this section ends on an extremely ominous note, as the morning sky is darkened by a violent storm. As setting is always connected to dramatic action and atmosphere in the world of *Great Expectations*, a storm can only mean that trouble lies ahead for Pip and his frightening benefactor.

CHAPTERS 40–46

SUMMARY: CHAPTER 40
In the morning, Pip trips over a shadowy man crouching on his staircase. He runs to fetch the watchman, but when they return the man is gone. Pip turns his attention to the convict, who gives his name as Abel Magwitch. To keep the servants from learning the truth, Pip decides to call Magwitch "Uncle Provis," an alias Magwitch made up for himself on the ship from Australia to England. Pip arranges a disguise and calls on Jaggers to confirm Magwitch's story. Magwitch tramps around the apartment, embarrassing Pip, "his" gentleman, with his bad table manners and rough speech.

SUMMARY: CHAPTER 41
After five days of enduring his guest, Pip is forced to confront his problem head-on when Herbert returns home. Magwitch leaves, and Herbert and Pip discuss the situation, agreeing that Pip should no longer use Magwitch's money. They plan for Pip to take Magwitch abroad, where he will be safe from the police, before parting ways with him.

SUMMARY: CHAPTER 42

The next morning, Magwitch tells the young men his story. He was an orphaned child and lived a life of crime out of necessity. His earliest memory is of stealing turnips to feed himself. As a young man, he met a gentleman criminal named Compeyson and fell under his power. Compeyson had already driven another accomplice, Arthur, into alcoholism and madness. Arthur, Magwitch says, was driven to despair by the memory of a wealthy woman he and Compeyson had once victimized. Magwitch remembers a woman from his own past and becomes distraught, but he does not tell Herbert and Pip about her. He continues, saying that when he and Compeyson were caught, Compeyson turned on him, using his gentleman's manners to obtain a light sentence at the trial. Magwitch wanted revenge, and Compeyson was the man Pip saw him struggling with that night on the marsh.

At this point, Herbert passes Pip a note that tangles the situation even further. The note reveals that Arthur was Miss Havisham's half brother; Compeyson was the man who stood her up on their wedding day.

SUMMARY: CHAPTER 43

Ashamed that his rise to social prominence is owed to such a coarse, lowborn man, Pip feels that he must leave Estella forever. After an unpleasant encounter with Drummle at the inn, he travels to Satis House to see Miss Havisham and Estella one final time.

SUMMARY: CHAPTER 44

Miss Havisham admits that she knowingly allowed him to believe she was his benefactor, and she agrees to help Herbert now that Pip can no longer use his own fortune. Pip finally tells Estella he loves her, but she coldly replies that she never deceived him into thinking she shared his feelings. She announces that she has decided to marry Drummle. Surprisingly, Miss Havisham seems to pity Pip.

Upset beyond words, Pip walks the whole way back to London. At a gate close to his home, a night porter gives him a note from Wemmick, reading "don't go home."

SUMMARY: CHAPTER 45

Afraid, Pip spends a night at a seedy inn called the Hummums. The next day, Pip finds Wemmick, who explains that he has learned through Jaggers's office that Compeyson is pursuing Magwitch. He says that Herbert has hidden Magwitch at Clara's house, and Pip leaves at once to go there.

SUMMARY: CHAPTER 46

Upon arriving, he finds that Clara's father is a drunken ogre and feels glad that he has helped Clara and Herbert escape him. He finds Magwitch upstairs and is surprised by the concern he now feels for the old convict's safety; he even shields Magwitch from the news of Compeyson's reappearance. Herbert and Pip discuss a plan to sneak Magwitch away on the river, and Pip begins to consider staying with his benefactor even after their escape. Pip buys a rowboat, keeping a nervous watch for the dark figure searching for Magwitch.

ANALYSIS: CHAPTERS 40–46

Throughout these chapters, Pip is again caught between powerful and conflicting feelings. When Joe visited London in Chapter 27, Pip was afraid both of how Joe would see his new life and of how the people in his new life would see Joe. Now, Pip is caught between his fear *of* Magwitch and his fear *for* Magwitch: he is afraid of the convict, but he also fears for Magwitch's safety. The news of Compeyson's arrival coincides with the appearance of the "man crouching in the corner" in the darkness on Pip's stairs, making the danger suddenly seem very real.

Magwitch's story of Compeyson also causes the two plotlines that have defined Pip's life—that of the convict and that of Miss Havisham and Estella—to collapse into one. This means that the world of Pip's secret guilt and the world of his highest aspiration share a common history, and the stark polarities in which Pip has always believed—the rigid lines separating good from evil and innocence from guilt—are suddenly threatened. Interestingly, when Pip goes to break off his relations with Estella and Miss Havisham in Chapter 44, only to find that Estella has abandoned him to marry Drummle, Miss Havisham seems to pity him. He says, "I saw Miss Havisham put her hand to her heart and hold it there, as she sat looking by turns at Estella and at me." Even as he tries to preserve his sense of their world by leaving it, protecting it from being tainted by the world of Magwitch, he finds Estella and Miss Havisham changing. Despite his efforts, his romantic ideals may be impossible to preserve.

The story of Compeyson also highlights the theme of class differences that has run throughout the novel. Magwitch is a low-born orphan, but Compeyson is an educated man. As Magwitch says in Chapter 42, "He set up fur a gentleman, this Compeyson . . . He was a smooth one to talk, and was a dab at the ways of gentle-folks." As a result, Compeyson was able to negotiate a light sentence at his trial, while the rough-edged Magwitch received a heavier one. Estella's cruelty spurred Pip to desire social status, but Compeyson's betrayal spurred Magwitch to desire something even more: Pip wished to become a gentleman, but Magwitch wished to "own" a gentleman, thus inspiring his plans for Pip.

Pip is fortunate throughout this section to have such good friends, emphasizing the novel's theme that loyalty and human affection are more important than social standing and ambition. Both Herbert and Wemmick are instrumental to the plot to rescue Magwitch. Herbert helps Pip from the beginning of the plan, and Wemmick even breaks the division between his office self and his Walworth self (subtly reflecting the collapse of other rigid categories throughout this section) to give Pip information about Compeyson that he learned at Jaggers's office.

Miss Havisham's softening toward Pip in this section is mirrored by Pip's gradual softening toward Magwitch. Though at first he seems fearsome and rough, the convict slowly impresses both Pip and Herbert with the raw sense of honor underneath his powerful personality. In Chapter 46, Magwitch seems kind and noble compared to Clara's brutish father, Bill Barley, and Pip is sincere when he tells him, "I don't like to leave you here." The subtle sense of suspicion and dread that seizes Pip's world—he cannot "get rid of the notion of being watched"—alarms him more for Magwitch's sake than it does for his own. He is in constant fear that Magwitch's pursuers are "going swiftly, silently, and surely to take him." The main mysteries of the novel (apart from that of Estella's parentage) have been resolved; Dickens now relies on a sense of suspense and danger to keep the plot moving forward.

CHAPTERS 47–52

SUMMARY: CHAPTER 47

Pip anxiously waits for Wemmick's signal to transport Magwitch downriver. Despite his softening attitude toward the convict, he feels morally obligated to refuse to spend any more of Magwitch's money, and his debts pile up. He realizes that Estella's marriage to Drummle must have taken place by now, but he intentionally avoids learning more about it. All of his worries are for Magwitch.

Pip goes to the theater to forget his troubles. After the performance, Wopsle tells Pip that in the audience behind him was one of the convicts from the battle on the marsh so many years ago. Pip tries to question Wopsle calmly, but inside he is terrified, realizing that Compeyson must be shadowing him. Pip rushes home to tell Herbert and Wemmick.

SUMMARY: CHAPTER 48

Jaggers invites Pip to dinner, where he gives the young man a note from Miss Havisham. When Jaggers mentions Estella's marriage shortly after Jaggers's housekeeper Molly walks in, Pip realizes that Molly is the person he couldn't place, the person Estella mysteriously resembles. He realizes at once that Molly must be Estella's mother. Walking home with Wemmick after the dinner, Pip questions his friend about Molly, and he learns that she was accused of killing a woman over her common-law husband and of murdering her little daughter to hurt him. Pip feels certain that Estella is that lost daughter.

SUMMARY: CHAPTER 49

Pip visits Miss Havisham, who feels unbearably guilty for having caused Estella to break his heart. Sobbing, she clings to Pip's feet, pleading with him to forgive her. He acts kindly toward her, then goes for a walk in the garden. There, he has a morbid fantasy that Miss Havisham is dead. He looks up at her window just in time to see her bend over the fire and go up in a column of flame. Rushing in to save her, Pip sweeps the ancient wedding feast from her table and smothers the flames with the tablecloth. Miss Havisham lives, but she becomes an invalid, a shadow of her former self. Pip stays with her after the doctors have departed; early the next morning, he leaves her in the care of her servants and returns to London.

SUMMARY: CHAPTER 50

Pip himself was badly burned trying to save Miss Havisham, and while Herbert changes his bandages, they agree that they have both grown fonder of Magwitch. Herbert tells Pip the part of Magwitch's story that the convict originally left out, the story of the woman in his past. The story matches that of Jaggers's housekeeper, Molly. Magwitch, therefore, is Molly's former common-law husband and Estella's father.

SUMMARY: CHAPTER 51

Pip is seized by a feverish conviction to learn the whole truth. He visits Jaggers and manages to shock the lawyer by proclaiming that he knows the truth of Estella's parentage. Pip cannot convince Jaggers to divulge any information, however, until he appeals to Wemmick's human, kind side, the side that until now Wemmick has never shown in the office. Jaggers is so surprised and pleased to learn that Wemmick has a pleasant side that he confirms that Estella is Molly's daughter, though he didn't know Magwitch's role in the story.

SUMMARY: CHAPTER 52

Pip leaves to finish the task of securing Herbert's partnership. He learns that Herbert is to be transferred to the Middle East, and Herbert fantasizes about escorting Clara to the land of Arabian Nights.

A message from Wemmick arrives, indicating that they should be ready to move Magwitch in two days. But Pip also finds an anonymous note threatening "Uncle Provis," demanding that Pip travel to the marshes in secret. Pip travels to the inn near his childhood home, where he is reminded of how badly he has neglected Joe since he became a gentleman. Of all his losses, Pip thinks he regrets the loss of Joe's friendship the most. That night, humbled and with an arm injured from the fire, he heads out to the mysterious meeting on the marshes.

ANALYSIS: CHAPTERS 47–52

Pip's compulsion to solve the mystery of Estella's origins fills him with a feverish purpose while he waits for Wemmick's signal. The story he uncovers connects even more completely the world of Miss Havisham and the world of Magwitch. Pip, who was originally mortified to learn that his fortune came from someone so far beneath Estella, now learns that Estella is the daughter of his secret benefactor and therefore springs from even humbler origins than himself. The revelation, nevertheless, does not seem to change his feelings for her. This is due in part to Pip's own changing feelings for Magwitch—Herbert and Pip are by this point loyal to the former convict—and in part to Pip's self-critical nature. He is still harder on himself than on those around him, and it is perfectly in keeping with his character to overlook in Estella something he could not overlook in himself.

Aside from the continuing progress of the plot to escape with Magwitch—evading Compeyson, waiting for Wemmick's signal—the most important development in this section is Miss Havisham's full repentance for her behavior toward Pip. The original dynamic between the two, with Miss Havisham as the manic, powerful old woman and Pip the cowering child, is completely reversed in Chapter 49, when Miss Havisham drops to her knees before Pip, crying, "What have I done! What have I done!" But something of Pip's original feeling for the dowager creeps back into his mind as he walks through the garden and imagines her hanging from a beam in the brewery, just as he used to do when he was a child.

When he looks through her bedroom window to reassure himself of her well-being, he sees her catching on fire and running at him, "shrieking, with a whirl of fire blazing all about her, and soaring at least as many feet above her head as she was high." Although her injuries from the fire leave her bedridden and destroyed (just as Orlick's attack left Mrs. Joe an invalid in Chapter 15), this dramatic ending to Miss Havisham's story does not assuage her guilt and remorse or end her search for Pip's forgiveness. From her bed, she continually entreats him, "Take a pencil and write under my name, 'I forgive her!'"

CHAPTERS 53–56

SUMMARY: CHAPTER 53

The night is dark over the marsh; in the sky the moon is a deep red. Thick mists surround the limekiln to which Pip travels. He enters an abandoned stone quarry and suddenly finds his candle extinguished; a noose is thrown over his head in the darkness. He is bound tightly, and a gruff voice threatens to kill him if he cries out. A flint is struck, its flame illuminating Orlick's wicked face.

Orlick accuses Pip of coming between him and a young woman he fancied, among other things, and declares his intention to have revenge. He also admits to killing Mrs. Joe, though he says that Pip is ultimately responsible for her death since Orlick did it to get back at him. "It was you, villain," Pip retorts boldly, but inside he is worried: he is afraid that he will die and none of his loved ones will know how he hoped to improve himself and to help them. Orlick reveals that he has some connection with Compeyson and has solved the mystery of Magwitch, and that he was the shadowy figure lurking in Pip's stairwell.

Orlick takes a swig of liquor, then picks up a stone hammer and advances menacingly toward Pip. Pip cries out, and suddenly Herbert bursts in with a group of men to save him. Herbert had found Orlick's note asking Pip to meet him at the marshes and, worried, had followed Pip there. In the ensuing scuffle, Orlick manages to escape. Rather than pursuing him, Pip rushes home with Herbert to carry out Magwitch's escape.

SUMMARY: CHAPTER 54

In the morning, a sparkling sunrise dazzles London as Pip and Herbert prepare to put their plan in motion. With their friend Startop, the pair set out on the river; the Thames is bustling with activity and crowded with boats. When they stop for Magwitch at Clara's house, he looks well and seems contemplative; he drags his hand in the water as the boat moves and compares life to a river. As they move out of London into the marshes, though, the mood darkens, the rowing becomes harder, and a sense of foreboding settles over the group. At the filthy inn where they stop that night, a servant tells them of an ominous boat he has seen lingering near the inn; Pip worries that it could be either the police or Compeyson. That night Pip sees two men looking into his boat, so the group arranges for Pip and Magwitch to sneak out early the next morning and rejoin the boat further down the river.

Making their way downriver, they see their goal—a German steamer that will take Pip and Magwitch away—in the distance. But suddenly another rowboat appears, and a policeman calls for Magwitch's arrest. Magwitch recognizes Compeyson on the other boat and dives into the river to attack him. They grapple, and each slips under the surface, but only Magwitch resurfaces. He claims not to have drowned Compeyson, though he says he would have liked to, but he cannot avoid being chained and led away to prison. Now completely loyal to him, Pip takes his hand and promises to stand by him.

SUMMARY: CHAPTER 55

Jaggers is certain that Magwitch will be found guilty, but Pip remains loyal. He does not worry when he learns that the state will appropriate Magwitch's fortune, including Pip's money. While Magwitch awaits sentencing, Herbert prepares to marry Clara and Wemmick enjoys a comical wedding to Miss Skiffins. Herbert offers Pip a job, but Pip delays his answer.

SUMMARY: CHAPTER 56

Pip visits Magwitch, who is sick and imprisoned, and works to free the stricken convict. But when the old man is found guilty and sentenced to death, as Jaggers had predicted, Magwitch tells the judge that he believes God has decreed his death as an act of forgiveness.

On the day of his death, he is too ill to speak. Pip eases his final moments by telling him that Estella—the child he believed to be lost—is alive, well, and a beautiful lady. Magwitch dies in peace, and Pip prays over his body, pleading with God to forgive his lost benefactor.

ANALYSIS: CHAPTERS 53–56

While the complex ambiguities of character have filled the previous chapters of *Great Expectations,* Orlick's untimely reappearance reintroduces an element of pure evil. Orlick has no redeeming qualities; he is malicious and cunning and hurts people simply because he enjoys it. He blames Pip for many things (for having ruined his chances with Biddy, causing him to be fired by Miss Havisham, and having always been favored by Joe), but his hatred for Pip is largely irrational: he simply wants to destroy him. "I won't have a rag of you, I won't have a bone of you, left on earth," he says in Chapter 53. Orlick seems to have no self-awareness and repeatedly refers to himself in the third person as "Old Orlick." In this way, Orlick contrasts powerfully with Pip, whose every action is subject to relentless self-scrutiny. If Pip, so aware of justice, punishment, and guilt everywhere he goes, represents an excess of reflection and self-judgment, Orlick represents a total lack of those qualities. He is a perfect tool for the manipulative Compeyson, who has no doubt orchestrated the entire attack.

In the world of *Great Expectations,* the brilliant sunrise that lights up the river the day of the escape attempt seems like a good omen. The trip down the Thames with Magwitch highlights the extent to which Pip has grown throughout the novel. The nervous, ambivalent child is now an adult confident in his actions, shepherding the once-terrifying Magwitch toward freedom.

Public and private morality are no longer one and the same for Pip and his friends. When they stop at the inn and learn of the ominous boat lingering outside, Pip's group is uncertain whom they should fear: the police or Compeyson—that is, the law or an outlaw. Ironically, they are captured by both, since Compeyson had gone to the police; when Magwitch discovers what he had done, the gentleman criminal's face is distorted by "white terror." Magwitch gets his revenge on Compeyson, even though he is not directly responsible for Compeyson's drowning. Unlike Pip's other former antagonists, such as Miss Havisham and Magwitch, Compeyson ends his life with an act of betrayal. The strict sense of justice that guides the novel demands that any sinful character will either be redeemed or come to a bad end. Pip is redeemed by his newfound love for his secret benefactor; Magwitch is redeemed by his inner nobility and love for Pip; and Miss Havisham is redeemed by her repentance. Though Magwitch and Miss Havisham die, they die at peace, while Compeyson simply disappears, and Orlick will be dragged to prison (see Chapter 57).

> "You had a child once, whom you loved and lost."
> *(See* QUOTATIONS, *p. 62)*

The way in which Magwitch dies in Chapter 56 is a testament to his own inner strength, and Pip's behavior immediately before Magwitch's death is a sign of his newfound love for the convict. Though Wemmick's comical wedding and Herbert's joyous engagement lighten the mood of tragedy in these concluding chapters, it is the manner of Magwitch's death—uncomplaining, believing death to be the reward of God's forgiveness—that renders his life a victory. The sunrise the morning of the escape attempt did not foretell a successful ending to Magwitch's escape attempt, but, instead, foreshadows his redemption in death. Pip has now completely accepted Magwitch as his "second father." As he says in Chapter 54: "For now my repugnance to him had all melted away, and in the hunted wounded shackled creature who held my hand in his, I only saw a man who had . . . felt affectionately, gratefully, and generously toward me with great constancy through a series of years." Pip is no longer concerned with social class: he simply sees that Magwitch has been better to him than he himself has been to Joe, signaling that Pip has at last learned the novel's greatest moral lesson. Loyalty, love, and human affection are more important than social class and material grandeur, and are the only goals worth striving for.

CHAPTERS 57–59

SUMMARY: CHAPTER 57

After Magwitch's death, Pip falls into a feverish illness. He is also arrested for debt and nearly carted away to prison; he is spared only because of his extreme ill health. He experiences wild hallucinations, reliving scenes with Orlick and Miss Havisham and continually seeing Joe's face. But the last is not a hallucination: Joe has really come, and he nurses Pip through his illness.

As Pip recovers, Joe tells him the news from home: Miss Havisham has died, wisely distributing her fortune among the Pockets.

After failing to kill Pip, Orlick robbed Pumblechook, and he since has been caught and put in jail. And Joe has news about himself: Biddy has helped him learn how to read and write.

Pip and Joe go on a Sunday outing, just as they used to do when Pip was a boy. But when Pip tries to tell Joe the story of Magwitch, Joe refuses to listen, not wanting to revisit painful memories. Despite Pip's renewed affection, living in London makes Joe increasingly unhappy, and one morning Pip finds him gone. Before leaving, he does Pip one last good turn, paying off all of Pip's debts. Pip rushes home to reconcile with Joe and decides to marry Biddy when he gets there.

SUMMARY: CHAPTER 58
When Pip arrives at his childhood home, he finds Satis House pulled apart in preparation for an auction. Pumblechook tracks him down at his hotel and treats him condescendingly, but Pip rudely takes his leave and goes to find Biddy and Joe. Biddy's schoolhouse is empty, as is Joe's smithy. When Pip finds them, he is shocked to discover that they have been married. Despite his disappointed expectation of marriage to Biddy, he expresses happiness for them and decides to take the job with Herbert.

SUMMARY: CHAPTER 59
Eleven years later, Pip returns to England. He says he has learned to work hard and is content with the modest living he makes in the mercantile firm. He goes to visit Joe and Biddy, and tries to convince Biddy that he has resigned himself to being a bachelor.

Pip then goes to Satis House and finds that it is no longer standing. In a silvery mist, Pip walks through the overgrown, ruined garden and thinks of Estella. He has heard that she was unhappy with Drummle but that Drummle has recently died. As the moon rises, Pip finds Estella wandering through the old garden. They discuss the past fondly; as the mists rise, they leave the garden hand in hand, Pip believes, never to part again.

ANALYSIS: CHAPTERS 57–59
The ending of *Great Expectations* is more controversial than it may seem at first. Before writing the scene in which Pip finds Estella in the garden and sees "no shadow of another parting from her," Dickens wrote another, less romantic ending to the book. In this version, Pip hears that, after Drummle's death, Estella married a country doctor in Shropshire. Walking through London one day with Joe and

Biddy's son, Pip runs into Estella and they have a very brief meeting and shake hands. Though they do not discuss the past, Pip says he could see that "suffering had been stronger than Miss Havisham's teaching and had given her a heart to understand what my heart used to be."

Dickens changed this ending at the suggestion of a friend, the novelist Edward Bulwer Lytton. He seems to have been motivated, at least in part, by the desire to please his reading public with a happy ending. Some critics have felt that the original ending of *Great Expectations* is more true to the tone of the novel, that the process of Pip's redemption as a character is exactly the process that would make his continued love for Estella impossible. Others have felt that the original ending is too harsh, that their common past has destined Pip and Estella for one another, and that the main story of the novel is the story of their mutual development toward the conditions in which their love can be realized.

There is no clear historical reason to favor one of these endings over the other. Dickens stuck with the final version through every subsequent edition of the novel, but the original ending, changed only through outside influence, was Dickens's first sense of how the story ought to end. Though the romantic ending remains the "official" ending of the book, each reader of *Great Expectations* may interpret the novel for him- or herself and decide which ending best fits his or her own understanding of the story.

In any case, Pip's fundamental development by this final section remains clear, and it is emphasized in his reconciliation with Joe and Biddy in Chapters 57 and 58. Here, the lessons Pip has learned effectively summarize the thematic development of the novel as a whole. Pip has learned that social class is not a criterion for happiness; that strict designations of good and evil, and even of guilt and innocence, are nearly impossible to maintain in a world that is constantly changing (symbolized by the destruction of Satis House, which attempted to freeze time with its stopped clocks); and that his treatment of his loved ones must be the guiding principle in his life. Though his self-description as a narrator shows that he continues to judge himself harshly, he has forgiven his enemies and been reconciled with his friends. Whether he leaves the garden with Estella or only bids her farewell in her carriage, he has found a satisfying ending for himself.

IMPORTANT QUOTATIONS EXPLAINED

1. My convict looked round him for the first time, and saw me
    . . . I looked at him eagerly when he looked at me, and
    slightly moved my hands and shook my head. I had been
    waiting for him to see me, that I might try to assure him of
    my innocence. It was not at all expressed to me that he even
    comprehended my intention, for he gave me a look that I did
    not understand, and it all passed in a moment. But if he had
    looked at me for an hour or for a day, I could not have
    remembered his face ever afterwards as having been more
    attentive.

This quote from Chapter 5 describes Pip's brief reunion with Magwitch after the latter has been captured by the police. Pip, who is always concerned with other people's impressions of his behavior, is anxious for Magwitch to know that he is innocent—that he is not responsible for turning Magwitch in to the police. But when Magwitch looks at Pip, he seems to experience feelings that have nothing to do with Pip's innocence or guilt, a look that Pip "did not understand" but which is the most "attentive" look Pip has ever received. This is an important moment of foreshadowing in the book, our first impression that Pip's kindness has moved Magwitch to strong feelings of loyalty and love. It also an important moment of character development, our first glimpse of something in Magwitch's character beyond the menace and bluster of his early scenes in the book.

2.   "Pip, dear old chap, life is made of ever so many partings
        welded together, as I may say, and one man's a blacksmith,
        and one's a whitesmith, and one's a goldsmith, and one's a
        coppersmith. Diwisions among such must come, and must
        be met as they come."

Joe says these words to Pip as a farewell in Chapter 27, after their
awkward meeting in London. Pip, now a gentleman, has been
uncomfortably embarrassed by both Joe's commonness and his own
opulent lifestyle, and the unpretentious Joe has felt like a fish out of
water in Pip's sumptuous apartment. With this quote, Joe tells Pip
that he does not blame him for the awkwardness of their meeting,
but he chalks it up instead to the natural divisions of life. The blacksmith concocts a metaphor of metalsmithing to describe these natural divisions: some men are blacksmiths, such as Joe, and some men
are goldsmiths, such as Pip. In these simple terms, Joe arrives at a
wise and resigned attitude toward the changes in Pip's social class
that have driven them apart, and he shows his essential goodness
and loyalty by blaming the division not on Pip but on the unalter-
able nature of the human condition.

3.   "I begin to think," said Estella, in a musing way, after
      another moment of calm wonder, "that I almost understand
      how this comes about. If you had brought up your adopted
      daughter wholly in the dark confinement of these rooms,
      and had never let her know that there was such a thing as the
      daylight by which she has never once seen your face—if you
      had done that, and then, for a purpose, had wanted her to
      understand the daylight and know all about it, you would
      have been disappointed and angry? . . ."

          "Or," said Estella, "—which is a nearer case—if you had
      taught her, from the dawn of her intelligence, with your
      utmost energy and might, that there was such a thing as
      daylight, but that it was made to be her enemy and
      destroyer, and she must always turn against it, for it had
      blighted you and would else blight her—if you had done
      this, and then, for a purpose, had wanted her to take
      naturally to the daylight and she could not do it, you would
      have been disappointed and angry? . . ."

          "So," said Estella, "I must be taken as I have been made.
      The success is not mine, the failure is not mine, but the two
      together make me."

Estella makes this speech to Miss Havisham in Chapter 38, when
Miss Havisham has complained that Estella treats her coldly and
without love. Astonished that her adopted mother would make
such an accusation after deliberately raising her to avoid emotional attachment and treat those who love her with deliberate
cruelty, Estella responds with this analytical exploration of Miss
Havisham's attitude. Using sunlight as a metaphor for love (an
appropriate metaphor, given Miss Havisham's refusal to go into
the sun), Estella first says that it is as if Miss Havisham raised her
without ever telling her about sunlight, then expected her to
understand it without having been taught. She then thinks of a
better metaphor and says that it is as if Miss Havisham did tell
her about sunlight, but told her that sunlight was her hated
enemy, then reacted with disappointment and anger when Estella
did not naturally love the sunlight.

    Estella concludes this metaphor by reminding Miss Havisham
that she made her as she is, and that Miss Havisham is responsible for her creation. Estella says that both Miss Havisham's "success" (Estella's coldness and cruelty) and her "failure" (Estella's

inability to express her emotions and inability to love) make her who she is. This quote is extremely important to Estella's development as a character, because it indicates her gradual arrival at self-knowledge, which will eventually enable her to overcome her past. The speech is also one of the best descriptions of Estella's character to be found in the book.

4.   "Look'ee here, Pip. I'm your second father. You're my son—
     more to me nor any son. I've put away money, only for you
     to spend. When I was a hired-out shepherd in a solitary hut,
     not seeing no faces but faces of sheep till I half-forgot wot
     men's and women's faces wos like, I see yourn. . . . I see you
     there a many times plain as ever I see you on them misty
     marshes. 'Lord strike me dead!' I says each time—and I goes
     out in the open air to say it under the open heavens—'but
     wot, if I gets liberty and money, I'll make that boy a
     gentleman!' And I done it. Why, look at you, dear boy! Look
     at these here lodgings of yourn, fit for a lord! A lord? Ah!
     You shall show money with lords for wagers, and beat 'em!'"

Magwitch makes this speech to Pip in Chapter 39, when he dramati-
cally reveals himself as Pip's secret benefactor and the source of all his
wealth. This revelation is crucially important to the plot of the novel, as
it collapses Pip's idealistic view of wealth and social class by forcing him
to realize that his own status as a gentleman is owed to the loyalty of a
lower-class criminal. The quote is also important for what it reveals
about Magwitch's character: previously, the convict has seemed menacing, mysterious, and frightening; with this quote, we receive our first
glimpse of his extraordinary inner nobility, manifested through the
powerful sense of loyalty he feels toward Pip.

QUOTATIONS

5.   "Dear Magwitch, I must tell you, now at last. You
       understand what I say?"
            A gentle pressure on my hand.
            "You had a child once, whom you loved and lost."
            A stronger pressure on my hand.
            "She lived and found powerful friends. She is living now.
       She is a lady and very beautiful. And I love her!"

In this passage from Chapter 56, Pip tells the dying Magwitch about
his daughter, Estella, whom he has not seen since she was a young
girl. If the arrival of Magwitch collapses Pip's idealistic view of the
upper classes, then the subsequent revelation that Estella—Pip's first
ideal of wealth and beauty—is the daughter of the convict buries it
for good. By consoling the dying Magwitch with the truth about
Estella, Pip shows the extent to which he has matured and developed a new understanding of what matters in life. Rather than
insisting on the idealistic hierarchy of social class that has been his
guiding principle in life, Pip is now able to see hierarchy as superficial and an insufficient guide to character. Loyalty, love, and inner
goodness are far more important than social designations, a fact
that Pip explicitly recognizes by openly acknowledging the compli-
cations that have made his former view of the world impossible.

KEY FACTS

FULL TITLE
Great Expectations

AUTHOR
Charles Dickens

TYPE OF WORK
Novel

GENRES
Bildungsroman, social criticism, autobiographical fiction

LANGUAGE
English

TIME AND PLACE WRITTEN
London, 1860-1861

DATE OF FIRST PUBLICATION
Published serially in England from December 1860 to August 1861; published in book form in England and America in 1861

PUBLISHER
Serialized in *All the Year Round*; published in England by Chapman & Hall; published in America by Harper & Brothers

NARRATOR
Pip

CLIMAX
A sequence of climactic events occurs from about Chapter 51 to Chapter 56: Miss Havisham's burning in the fire, Orlick's attempt to murder Pip, and Pip's attempt to help Magwitch escape London.

PROTAGONIST
Pip

ANTAGONIST

Great Expectations does not contain a traditional single antagonist. Various characters serve as figures against whom Pip must struggle at various times: Magwitch, Mrs. Joe, Miss Havisham, Estella, Orlick, Bentley Drummle, and Compeyson. With the exception of the last three, each of the novel's antagonists is redeemed before the end of the book.

SETTING (TIME)

Mid-nineteenth century

SETTINGS (PLACE)

Kent and London, England

POINT OF VIEW

First person

FALLING ACTION

The period following Magwitch's capture in Chapter 54, including Magwitch's death, Pip's reconciliation with Joe, and Pip's reunion with Estella eleven years later

TENSE

Past

FORESHADOWING

Great Expectations contains a great deal of foreshadowing. The repeated references to the convict (the man with the file in the pub, the attack on Mrs. Joe) foreshadow his return; the second convict on the marsh foreshadows the revelation of Magwitch's conflict with Compeyson; the man in the pub who gives Pip money foreshadows the revelation that Pip's fortune comes from Magwitch; Miss Havisham's wedding dress and her bizarre surroundings foreshadow the revelation of her past and her relationship with Estella; Pip's feeling that Estella reminds him of someone he knows foreshadows his discovery of the truth of her parentage; the fact that Jaggers is a criminal lawyer foreshadows his involvement in Magwitch's life; and so on. Moreover, the weather often foreshadows dramatic events: a storm brewing generally means there will be trouble ahead, as on the night of Magwitch's return.

KEY FACTS

TONE

Comic, cheerful, satirical, wry, critical, sentimental, dark, dramatic, foreboding, Gothic, sympathetic

THEMES

> Ambition and the desire for self-improvement (social, economic, educational, and moral); guilt, criminality, and innocence; maturation and the growth from childhood to adulthood; the importance of affection, loyalty, and sympathy over social advancement and class superiority; social class; the difficulty of maintaining superficial moral and social categories in a constantly changing world

MOTIFS

Crime and criminality; disappointed expectations; the connection between weather or atmosphere and dramatic events; doubles (two convicts, two secret benefactors, two invalids, etc.)

SYMBOLS

The stopped clocks at Satis House symbolize Miss Havisham's attempt to stop time; the many objects relating to crime and guilt (gallows, prisons, handcuffs, policemen, lawyers, courts, convicts, chains, files) symbolize the theme of guilt and innocence; Satis House represents the upper-class world to which Pip longs to belong; Bentley Drummle represents the grotesque caprice of the upper class; Joe represents conscience, affection, loyalty, and simple good nature; the marsh mists represent danger and ambiguity.

KEY FACTS

STUDY QUESTIONS & ESSAY TOPICS

STUDY QUESTIONS

1. *Discuss Pip as both a narrator and a character. How are different aspects of his personality revealed by his telling of his story and by his participation in the story itself?*

Pip's story—the story of the novel—traces his development through the events of his early life; his narration, however, written years after the end of the story, is a product of his character as it exists *after* the events of the story. Pip's narration thus reveals the psychological endpoint of his development in the novel. Pip's behavior as a character often reveals only part of the story—he treats Joe coldly, for instance—while his manner as a narrator completes that story: his guilt for his poor behavior toward his loved ones endures, even as he writes about his early life years later. Of course, Dickens manipulates Pip's narration in order to evoke its subjects effectively: Pip's childhood is narrated in a much more childlike voice than his adult years, even though the narrator Pip presumably writes both parts of the story at a single later date. Dickens also uses Pip's narration to reinforce particular aspects of his character that emerge in the course of the novel: we know from his actions that Pip is somewhat self-centered but sympathetic at heart to others; Pip's later narration of his relationships with others tends to reflect those qualities. When Magwitch reveals that he is Pip's benefactor, for instance, Pip is disgusted by the convict and describes him solely in negative terms; as his affection for Magwitch grows, the descriptive terms he chooses to apply to the convict become much more positive.

2. *What role does social class play in* GREAT
    EXPECTATIONS? *What lessons does Pip learn from his
    experience as a wealthy gentleman? How is the theme of
    social class central to the novel?*

One way to see Pip's development, and the development of many of
the other characters in *Great Expectations,* is as an attempt to learn
to value other human beings: Pip must learn how to value Joe and
Magwitch, Estella must learn how to value Pip, and so on. Throughout the novel, social class provides an arbitrary, external standard of
value by which the characters (particularly Pip) judge one another.
Because social class is rigid and preexisting, it is an attractive standard for every character who lacks a clear conscience with which to
make judgments—Mrs. Joe and Pumblechook, for instance. And
because high social class is associated with romantic qualities such
as luxury and education, it is an immediately attractive standard of
value for Pip. After he is elevated to the status of gentleman, though,
Pip begins to see social class for what it is: an unjust, capricious standard that is largely incompatible with his own morals. There is simply no reason why Bentley Drummle should be valued above Joe,
and Pip senses that fact. The most important lesson Pip learns in the
novel—and perhaps the most important theme in *Great Expectations*—is that no external standard of value can replace the judgments of one's own conscience. Characters such as Joe and Biddy
know this instinctively; for Pip, it is a long, hard lesson, the learning
of which makes up much of the book.

3.   *Throughout the novel, Pip is plagued by powerful feelings of guilt and shame, and everywhere he goes he tends to encounter symbols of justice—handcuffs, gallows, prisons, and courtrooms. What is the role of guilt in the novel? What does it mean to be "innocent"?*

At the beginning of the novel, Pip's feelings of conscience are determined largely by his fear of what others might think, a state of mind no doubt reinforced by Mrs. Joe's "Tickler." He has strong feelings of guilt but an inadequate system by which to judge right and wrong; unable to determine the value of his own actions, he feels guilty even when he does the right thing. He acts with compassion and sympathy when he helps the convict, but he nevertheless feels deeply guilty and imagines that the police are waiting to take him away. As the novel progresses, Pip comes closer to trusting his own feelings; when he helps Magwitch at the end of the novel, he feels no guilt, only love, and he remains with the convict even after the police arrive to take him away. Throughout the novel, symbols of justice, such as prisons and police, serve as reminders of the questions of conscience that plague Pip: just as social class provides an external standard of value irrespective of a person's inner worth, the law provides an external standard of moral behavior irrespective of a person's inner feelings. Pip's wholehearted commitment to helping Magwitch escape the law in the last section of the novel contrasts powerfully with his childhood fear of police and shows that, though he continues to be very hard on his own shortcomings, Pip has moved closer to a reliance on his own inner conscience—which is the only way, as Joe and Biddy show, that a character can truly be "innocent."

QUESTIONS & ESSAYS

SUGGESTED ESSAY TOPICS

1. What significance does the novel's title, GREAT EXPECTATIONS, have for the story? In what ways does Pip have "great expectations"?

2. For much of GREAT EXPECTATIONS, Pip seems to believe in a stark division between good and evil, and he tends to classify people and situations as belonging to one extreme or the other: for instance, despite their respective complexities, he believes that Estella is good and the convict is evil. Yet, both socially and morally, Pip himself is often caught between extremes; his own situation rarely matches up to his moral vision. What is the role of moral extremes in this novel? What does it mean to be ambiguous or caught between extremes?

3. Discuss the character of Miss Havisham. What themes does she embody? What experiences have made her as she is? Is she a believable character? How does she relate to Pip and Estella?

4. Think about the novel's two endings—the "official" version in which Pip and Estella are reunited in the garden and the earlier version in which they merely speak briefly on the street and go their separate ways. Which version do you prefer? Which version seems more true to the thematic development of the novel? Why?

Review & Resources

Quiz

1. What is the name of Miss Havisham's manor?

   A. Satis House
   B. Lockmont
   C. Larchmont
   D. Satyr House

2. In what region of England are the marshes of the novel found?

   A. Sussex
   B. Wessex
   C. Kent
   D. Gloucestershire

3. How old is Pip when Magwitch returns to his life?

   A. 9
   B. 23
   C. 18
   D. 7

4. In what publication was *Great Expectations* originally serialized?

   A. *Home and Away*
   B. *The English Almanac*
   C. *Simple Wisdom*
   D. *All the Year Round*

5. To what genre of fiction, defined by its depiction of a character's growth from childhood to adulthood, does *Great Expectations* belong?

    A. Bildungsroman
    B. Kunstlerspiegel
    C. Mannerism
    D. Victorian paternalism

6. Who is Pip's tutor in London?

    A. Harold Pocket
    B. Walter Pocket
    C. Herbert Pocket
    D. Matthew Pocket

7. Who is Estella's father?

    A. Compeyson
    B. Magwitch
    C. Joe
    D. Jaggers

8. What action does Jaggers perform obsessively?

    A. He straightens his necktie
    B. He adjusts his hair
    C. He signs his name
    D. He washes his hands

9. What is Pip's reaction to Joe's visit to him in London?

    A. Embarrassment
    B. Joy
    C. Anger
    D. Resignation

10. Who takes credit for Pip's rise in social status?

    A. Mrs. Joe
    B. Joe
    C. Pumblechook
    D. Biddy

REVIEW & RESOURCES

11. Who is responsible for the attack on Mrs. Joe?

    A. Magwitch
    B. Orlick
    C. Compeyson
    D. Pip

12. For most of the novel, whom does Pip suspect of being his secret benefactor?

    A. Jaggers
    B. Magwitch
    C. Joe
    D. Miss Havisham

13. What name does Wemmick call his elderly father?

    A. "Aged Parent"
    B. "Venerable Ancestor"
    C. "Decrepit Sire"
    D. "Old Feller"

14. Who tells Pip that Compeyson was Miss Havisham's fiancé?

    A. Wemmick
    B. Estella
    C. Herbert
    D. Magwitch

15. What is Herbert's nickname for Pip?

    A. Haydn
    B. Handel
    C. Mendelssohn
    D. Salieri

16. Where does Pip first encounter Magwitch?

    A. The river
    B. Mrs. Joe's house
    C. The smithy
    D. The churchyard

REVIEW & RESOURCES

17. Who is the "pale young gentleman"?

    A.   Wemmick

    B.   Herbert

    C.   Jaggers

    D.   Startop

18. Whom does Estella marry?

    A.   Startop

    B.   Pip

    C.   Drummle

    D.   Herbert

19. Who buys Herbert's way into business?

    A.   Pip

    B.   Miss Havisham

    C.   Drummle

    D.   Estella

20. What happens to Compeyson at the end of the novel?

    A.   He escapes with the Havisham fortune

    B.   He is shot by the police

    C.   He is killed by Orlick

    D.   He disappears and is presumed drowned

21. Where does Estella live when she goes abroad?

    A.   France

    B.   Spain

    C.   Germany

    D.   Boston

22. What was the name of Miss Havisham's brother, Compeyson's first partner?

    A.   Magwitch

    B.   Tumbler

    C.   Arthur

    D.   John

23. What accident befalls Miss Havisham before her death?

    A. She is thrown from a horse
    B. She falls from a window
    C. A table crushes her legs
    D. She is burned in a fire

24. What is the source of the Havisham fortune?

    A. Lumberyards
    B. A cotton mill
    C. A brewery
    D. A noble estate

25. What code name do Pip and Herbert devise for Magwitch?

    A. Provis
    B. Clovis
    C. Quo Vadis
    D. Uncle Caveat

SUGGESTIONS FOR FURTHER READING

CHESTERTON, G. K. *Appreciations and Criticisms of the Works of Charles Dickens.* New York: Dutton, 1911.

COLLINS, PHILIP. *Dickens and Education.* New York: St. Martins, 1963.

DICKENS, CHARLES. *Great Expectations.* New York: Bantam, 1986.

LEAVIS, F. R., and Q. D. LEAVIS. *Dickens the Novelist.* London: Chatto and Windus, 1970.

MANNING, SYLVIA BANK. *Dickens as Satirist.* New Haven: Yale University Press, 1971.

WILSON, ANGUS. *The World of Charles Dickens.* New York: Viking, 1970.

WILSON, EDMUND. *The Wound and the Bow: Seven Studies in Literature.* Boston: Houghton Mifflin, 1941.

SPARKNOTES
TEST PREPARATION
GUIDES

The SparkNotes team figured it was time to cut standardized tests down to size. We've studied the tests for you, so that SparkNotes test prep guides are:

Smarter:
Packed with critical-thinking skills and test-
taking strategies that will improve your score.

Better:
Fully up to date, covering all new features of the tests,
with study tips on every type of question.

Faster:
Our books cover exactly what you need to
know for the test. No more, no less.

SparkNotes Guide to the SAT & PSAT
SparkNotes Guide to the SAT & PSAT—Deluxe Internet Edition
SparkNotes Guide to the ACT
SparkNotes Guide to the ACT—Deluxe Internet Edition
SparkNotes Guide to the SAT II Writing
SparkNotes Guide to the SAT II U.S. History
SparkNotes Guide to the SAT II Math Ic
SparkNotes Guide to the SAT II Math IIc
SparkNotes Guide to the SAT II Biology
SparkNotes Guide to the SAT II Physics

SparkNotes Literature Guides